OLDER, WISER, FIERCER

THE WISDOM COLLECTION

CAROL ORSBORN, PH.D.

Winner of Gold, Nautilus Book Awards, Consciously Aging

FIERCE
w/ Age

Fierce with Age Press
www.FierceWithAge.com
Nashville, Tennessee

ISBN: 1079544992
ISBN-13: 978-1079544992
Copyright © 2019 by Carol Orsborn

Author's Note: This is a work of nonfiction. In order to protect the privacy of individuals featured in the entries, some names, descriptions and locations have been altered. A number of these essays appeared previously at CarolOrsborn.com.

About the Cover Art: "Bouquet From The Side Garden" by Susan Rios.

Permission to use the cover painting in conjunction with this work is granted by Susan Rios. Sharing, duplication or dissemination in any way by written permission of the artist only. *Susan Rios Designs www.susanriosdesigns.com and www.susanriosdesigns.etsy.com*

To the Fierce Ones

who walked the path before us lighting the way

CONTENTS

FOREWORD   xi
Through the Gate
Harry R. Moody, Ph.D.

INTRODUCTION   1
An Arrival

I. We Who Are Old   5
The true nature of aging to those of us living it

    What Is Age?   6
    A Private Pleasure   8
    Beyond Power   10
    Growing Wild   14
    Catching the Breeze   16
    The Second Mile   18
    On Enduring   20
    Milestone Birthday   23
    The Senses   26
    Three Octogenarians   28

II. Legacy of Being   31
Anticipated regret and unexpected passion

    In the Gap   32

A Vision   34
The Happy Ghost   38
The Facts of Life   42
Garbed in Holiness   44
Confession   49

III. Our Times   53
The state of the world in our culminating
    moment

Jaws Agape   54
Not Too Late   56
Rear-View Mirror   59
Lock-Step   62
Advances   64
Human Potential   66
Whitewash   68

IV. The Paradox of Relatedness   73
The tension between wanting to belong and
    the desire for solitude

The Risk   74
Do Not Disturb   77
Gestation   79
Breathing Space   81
Mulch   83
A Glorious End   86

Called to Struggle   88
A New Season   90

V. Defeat and Victory   95
What is lost, what is gained through aging

Candidates   96
A Tender Shoot   99
Disassembling   101
The Source   103
Protest   106
For St. Joseph   108
Great Adventure   111

VI. Fierce with Age   115
Growing not only old but whole

Grand Gesture   116
Beyond Resignation   118
Becoming Yourself   120
Flooded   122
Sacred Identity   124
This Patch   126
Claiming Joy   129
Silence   131
Houseboat   133
Eclipse   135
Wonderfully Made   137

VII. That I May Smile Again   141
When life matters most

Doggy Steps   142
The Friendly Mirror   145
Fallible   148
Field of Love   150
Stray   154
Next Breath   158
Arrival   161
Head-First   164
One White Crane   167

AFTERWORD   169
Work of Art
Robert L. Weber, Ph.D.

ACKNOWLEDGMENTS   173

APPENDICES   175

Biographies   176
Stay Connected   184
Related Books by Carol Orsborn   186

FOREWORD
THROUGH THE GATE
Harry R. Moody, Ph.D.

The great critic Ananda Coomaraswamy once said, it's not that the artist is a special kind of person, it's that each person is a special kind of artist. Among many great artists, there comes a time when it is no longer necessary to promote their art or to achieve something. We see this process in many great artists from Rembrandt to Georgia O'Keefe, from Renoir to Kathe Kollwitz. German scholars long ago gave it a name: "*spaete Werke*" (late work) and also "*spaete Freiheit*" (late freedom). The Jungians have their word for it: "Individuation," or "becoming the person you were meant to be."

This is the theme, the touchstone that we find repeatedly in *Older, Wiser, Fiercer*. What the elder artists disclosed through paint, Carol Orsborn discloses to us through her words: "Now that I am old . . . I have gone all in on who I really am, availing myself anew to self-exposure. But this time my response is different: a growing bolder rather than shrinking back. I am not being careful anymore. I am growing wild." How grateful I am that she has reclaimed those words: "Now that I am old…"

I find this message delivered in a different way in one of the great novels about old age: *A Christmas Carol* by Charles Dickens, where the hero, Ebenezer Scrooge, goes on a dream journey, from despair to affirmation, in a single night. But Scrooge's journey begins, and is powered, by disillusionment. So it is in Carol Orsborn's journey, which is, in part, the voice of a generation. She is among the oldest of the now aging Boomers: "Our generation did everything in our power to gain control over our circumstances, individual as well as societal. Is this true of every generation? If so, the old have been, are and will always be doomed to failure."

Like the elders who came before her, like May Sarton, Zalman Schachter-Shalomi, Florida Scott-Maxwell, Thomas Merton and so many others who have pointed the way forward, Carol Orsborn does not shy away from the acknowledgment of failure. Paradoxically, this is the core recognition that comprises the essence of "conscious aging"—an overturning of the Boomer definition of success that has driven her generation through the years. As Orsborn puts it: "How ironic that now that I am old—after all these years striving to be Someone—I am once again not the point." Our contemporary master of old age, Baba Ram Dass, spoke at the first conference on conscious aging and charged all who were there (I was one) by saying "Aging is the school of nobody-ness. You have to enroll in that school." Ram Dass was echoing the words of Emily Dickinson when she wrote: "I'm nobody. Who are you? Are you nobody, too?" The paradox here is that it is in this very recognition of our nobody-ness that we have the potential to experience something even greater than the success for which we strived.

Another great contemporary master of aging was the psychologist James Hillman, who titled his book on the subject *The Force of Character and the Lasting Life*. Character is what shines out through all the pages of *Older, Wiser, Fiercer*: "Call it character—that mix of acceptance, courage, and perseverance that for many of us grow in tandem with the losses," she writes. Again and again, Orsborn drills down into herself and returns to the surface with paradoxes "that defy the rational and force me open-eyed into faith." Yes, Orsborn has written a book about faith, but it is not about religion as we typically understand it. Conscious aging is also about this faith, which takes different forms in different people, as we see in the great artists in old age. But all forms, as Orsborn says, are about something greater than happiness: about being intensely alive. "This is not the understanding of success promised by Boomer optimism nor is it a transcendence of life's messiness.

Rather it is a plunging in: heartbreaking and disturbing, piercing, joyful, and alive," she writes.

You will find many glimpses of Carol Orsborn's life in these essays: her dogs, the boat where she retreats for solitude, her pondering of great texts. But this collection is not the "Carol Orsborn" story. On the contrary, it is about how she outgrows her own story, which is itself the message of conscious aging: "In place of comparison or competition, our individual stories recede and awe advances."

Like all the great voyagers, Carol Orsborn has brought back to us, not a story of her travels, but a gift which can belong to us if only we summon the courage to follow in her footsteps. Indeed, it is not about comparison or competition at all. In the words of Jalal ad-Din Rumi: "Inside the Great Mystery that is, we don't really own anything. What is this competition we feel then, before we go, one at a time, through the same gate?" Carol Orsborn has written a remarkable classic, a worthy addition to the growing body of conscious aging literature. It is an unbelievable privilege to engage with what she's given here to me and to the world.

INTRODUCTION
AN ARRIVAL

Welcome to *Older, Wiser, Fiercer: The Wisdom Collection*, the culmination of my lifework in the field of conscious aging. In the pages following, you will encounter my evolving meditations and commentary about the true nature of aging to those of us living it, rooted in questions and building toward an arrival. Along the way I share a sequenced collection of essays that capture in real time growing older as an experience of paradox in which one has the potential to be at one moment stumbling along on shaky ground and at the next leaping upwards on fire with life.

Under the best of circumstances, growing older represents a disruption of how things used to be. This is a particularly difficult message for our generation of Boomers coming into age. We are a cohort who are used to thinking of ourselves as getting our own way, and who are now struggling with both individual and societal disillusionment. It is clear that our world needs wise elders more than ever. More than this, we who have lived long and well must become the wise elders. But how shall we accomplish this in our unexpectedly perilous times?

Immersed as I have been all my life in my generation, as both a thought leader and member, I knew I needed someone from outside the system of generational attitudes to shake me awake from assumptions I did not even know I held. Eight years ago, following the publication of my own coming into age book *Fierce with Age: Chasing God and Squirrels in Brooklyn*, I founded *Fierce with Age: the Digest of Boomer Wisdom, Inspiration and Spirituality* in order to immerse myself in the wisdom of elders from other generations and across a wide spectrum of eras and traditions and to share my discoveries with others. I found my inspiration in the likes of Ram Dass, Zalman Schachter-Shalomi, Joan Chittister, Connie Goldman, Rumi, Parker J. Palmer, and May Sarton, and in the woman I have come to think of as my soul sister, Jungian author Florida Scott-Maxwell, who fifty years ago, in her mid-eighties published her classic on aging *The Measure of My Days*. Here were psychologists, spiritual thinkers, philosophers, and mystics, past and present, who across the board warned against romanticized notions of aging as complacency. Rather, they dove head-first into a level of authenticity to which I aspire, revealing an experience of aging that is at once heartbreaking and disturbing, piercing, joyful, and alive.

This is not the understanding of success promised by Boomer optimism nor is it a transcendence of life's messiness. Rather it is a plunging in. The deeper I read into these elders' work, the clearer it became that I wanted to think about the things they were thinking about, at the depths of their consideration, and to evolve to a new level of maturity.

These essays, *Older, Wiser, Fiercer: The Wisdom Collection*, are the result: a creative act that is part interpretive jazz, part Midrash. *Older, Wiser, Fiercer* is both a living document—an interactive response to elders who have walked the path ahead of us—and a daring dive into my own experience of conscious aging. Faithful readers of my blog over the years will recognize many evolving themes as I've crafted 20 years of writing on the subject of spirituality and age into a culminating body of work.

It is my hope that *Older, Wiser, Fiercer: The Wisdom Collection* joins the growing body of conscious aging literature paying testimony to the human spirit through the entire cycle of seasons. Like life itself, conscious aging is a perilous journey that can at the same time be wrenchingly honest and passionately alive, if only we let it.

I
WE WHO ARE OLD
The true nature of aging to those of us living it

WHAT IS AGE?

What is age to those of us living it? Having crossed the threshold into my seventies, I am filled with equal portions of wonder and dread. The young cannot possibly fathom what it means to live with one's cheek pressed hard against the shadows. Earlier in our lives, we had expected either to continue on as is forever, punctuated by a hard stop at the end, or to fade away gently into the dark night. We did not anticipate facing a new threshold at this age, feeling more alive than ever. The irony nearly breaks us, as we leapfrog through the mystery of age one paradox at a time.

Aging is a time full of irony. We find ourselves brimming with unexpected passion, but frequently lack the energy to see things through. We experience ourselves to be at the peak of our knowledge and abilities, only to realize that we are masters of a world that no longer exists. At times we are full of purpose; other times we wonder what it has all been for.

We who are old discover untapped reservoirs of compassion for humanity while having less patience for acquaintances than ever before. We crave to be included while yearning for solitude—to be desperately wanted but desiring only to be left alone. We are fearful we won't have enough for the demands of the cavernous future that lies ahead while dreading the possibility that tomorrow may be our last. There is nothing quiescent or settled about any of this, even should there be moments or even long stretches of indescribable peace and joy.

But it doesn't last, and our righteous indignation is well justified—if useless. We're often uncertain how much more we can bear. And yet we pray with every fiber of our being for more.

A PRIVATE PLEASURE

Aging cedes territory on a daily basis. Every day we are somewhat weaker, somewhat slower, somewhat less connected. The only thing that comprises "more" for us is the effort it now takes to try to maintain what came to us so effortlessly just moments ago. The slippage is often so slow and slight, we become used to accepting that we have been changed before we notice what happened. But surrendering does not diminish the fact that there is pain involved.

The stage in life where one can become larger than one's losses is over—no pushing through, battling or overcoming will have ever proven, in the end, to have

8

been enough. Only when we let ourselves become smaller than our losses—when we grant ourselves permission to curl up in mute silence alongside our pain—can we find peace.

This does not happen suddenly or dramatically, so we will not notice a particular moment when we give up trying to overcome our difficulties and rather come to rest in God's tender embrace. This is not an experience to be shared with others, but a private pleasure one prefers to keep to oneself.

BEYOND POWER

Sometimes I am grateful for all the years of my life, believing that they have grown me strong. Other times, I wear them as gravity, weighing me down: everything sinking. On these days, upon awakening, I can feel I haven't rested enough. Even without a mirror nearby, I can sense it: perhaps not as a physical truth but as a matter of spirit. My body, my energy, my world. I am not who I used to be.

This is not necessarily a bad thing. When left to our own devices, our tendency is to rely on attitudes and actions that at least hold the promise of mastery. Our society thinks of this as vitality, creativity, and power. And for most of our lives, we have been clever enough to build constructions meant to shield us from the truth that sooner or later, we are bound to come face to face with our limitations.

By the time we are old, we have lived long enough to know what we and the world are capable of: the heights to which we can rise, and the depths to which we can sink. If at that point we allow ourselves to break open rather than shore up, we have the potential to live deeper, more authentically—sometimes for worse, often for better. Perhaps evolution has given us old age because it takes so long to get beyond denying, defending, and story-telling to live life in its intended intensity.

It takes inner courage and faith to willingly engage in the struggle to face our shadows and become more conscious of the greater truth of what is really going on at any moment. Few of us become willing to take on the potential for the pain of awakening before we have attempted every apparent shortcut—and there are many. It takes not years but most of one's life to exhaust the alternatives, realizing that over and over again we have fooled ourselves into thinking that there are easier ways to go.

At long last, we run out of options, panting across the boundary to this new land, inhabited by a handful of others like us: old, brave souls who are struggling to become not only older and wiser, but fiercer. To be old and awake is to be granted fresh sight, informed by humility, perspective and compassion—for self and for others. We who have been so relentlessly busy trying to make things right for ourselves, our loved ones, and the world, may now just as likely be found sitting for long spells in silence.

Others may misinterpret this as emptiness, but we are not devoid of anything. In fact, if anything, there is too much. Awe, grief, joy, mystery, righteous anger, fresh insight, renewed conviction, humility, hope, despair. Each takes a turn and often they are happening all at once.

I could try to go back to sleep, but our beloved senior dogs, Lucky, Molly, and Sammy, are restless and I know that entering this day is a choice I must make. I am prepared for the worst, just when I'm caught off-guard by a beam of sunlight, warming the bend in my arm that happens to be pillowing Lucky's watchful head. Her tail is wagging so fast, the bed shakes. Suddenly, I need do nothing more than feel.

GROWING WILD

Our generation did everything in our power to gain control over our circumstances, individual as well as societal. Is this true of every generation? If so, the old have been, are, and will always be doomed to failure. But failure, as it turns out, can provide rich ground for surprises.

I am freshly exposed at this new age and stage of life to be as vulnerable as a child who has lost her innocence. The child, growing through adolescence into adulthood, has ample time to try on various personas offering protective cover, until she finds one that fits well enough. I remember the relief I once felt when I figured out who and how I could be that would cause the least friction with others. This well-honed persona was one that allowed me maximum room to nurture if not the whole, at least the core, of the seed of my authentic self.

Now that I am old, the seed has taken over. I have gone all in on who I really am, availing myself anew to self-exposure. The persona is no longer functioning as I once hoped it would—offering the cover of protection as part of an ongoing, diligent work in progress. But this time my response to self-exposure is different: a growing bolder rather than shrinking back. I am not being careful anymore. I am growing wild.

CATCHING THE BREEZE

When I was young, my sails often filled with air. Even now, some days are effortless as I race across the surface of the hours overflowing with more life than I know what to do with. Other days, I pull at the ropes hoping to catch just enough wind to keep moving forward: just engaged, active, caring, courageous enough.

And then there are the days when there is no breeze to capture at all. But even these days, if I don't make a fuss about the way things used to or could be, can be sweeter than I'd ever imagined.

Just yesterday, I was zipping along in full sail. I enjoyed the energy, the purposefulness. At the same time, there was a sense of freedom because I did not worry that the wind might change direction or die down.

When we are young, we need billowing sails because we have so many miles to go. I don't need as much now—just as much as necessary. The slightest breeze can be more welcomed and appreciated in older age than the great blasts of energy we previously enjoyed. But this comes about only once we avail ourselves to drifting through the sweet joy of life, no longer worrying about where we must get to.

THE SECOND MILE

I went to the neighborhood senior center for my usual workout. I am continually amazed both that I am old enough to be allowed into such a place—and humbled by how much better the eighty-year-olds can be than me at reaching the floor with their palms and balancing on one leg.

But today when I arrived, there was someone new. Settled heavily on the sit-up bench huddled an old man whose body was wide and inert. My mind could not make sense of where he ended and his sweat clothes began, piling about him on the bench like a mound of unsorted laundry.

But then, by chance, our eyes met and we shared in that fleeting moment something unspoken but important. An understanding.

He hoisted himself up and walked one labored step at a time towards the treadmill.

"My second mile of the day," he said. Then we nodded to one another with utmost respect.

Increasingly, I encounter others my age and older who along with physical diminishment emanate the aura of self-acceptance. We may not run marathons any more, but we do what we can. And when we do, we radiate. I am humbled in the presence of this numinous beauty—not the prettiness of the young, but expressive of something the young cannot duplicate. It is as if time has the potential to erode us into something wondrous. This is a transformation that cannot be forced, only allowed.

ON ENDURING

When I was younger, I did not think it possible to embrace a deficit that could not be corrected, a problem that could not be solved, a loss that could not be overcome. God knows, I attempted everything. For long stretches, I kept my eyes so focused on the goal, I inadvertently blinded myself to much of the incremental good that lined the way. When I fell short anyway, I thought it was my fault or found some way to place the blame on others.

But this angst can be temporary, if only one becomes willing to accept that there is nothing one can do that will forestall nature's entropy indefinitely.

One would think this would doom one to live the remainder of one's life in distress. But in my experience, the angst came earlier—in that transitional stage where effort, guilt, and remorse accompanied every trip to the mirror. Eventually, exhausting every possible attempt to achieve perfection, I gave up. And yet I endured.

It takes a long time to burn through the layers of self-protection. But persist long enough and the dross will eventually reveal an ember glowing through the charred remains of denial. One can wait a very long time for this glimmer of the holy—something that persists in us that has nothing to do with age, death, or anything that could possibly ever be lost.

What a relief when we come to realize that age viewed through the lens of character means that we no longer have to submit ourselves to judgment or work for compliments. What does it matter anymore whether one was once the most or least popular? The one who won the races or, despite one's personal best, came in last? After a lifetime of effort, how glorious to no longer feel compelled to compete with others. Who would have ever believed that one could not only get used to it, but relish it?

MILESTONE BIRTHDAY

Over the years, I've come to embrace aging as a gift and privilege: the growing freedom, the welcome lessening of ego, the early signs of wisdom. Then turning 70 snuck up on me. Things began simply enough, making plans to celebrate my milestone birthday. But it got complicated. First, a good friend who'd thought she could be with me on the big day had to cancel. Shortly thereafter, I found myself unable to stop dropping hints about gift ideas to my husband. Then I called several friends to talk about things that were suddenly consuming me. Troublesome decisions by others that hadn't yet been made; a cold that could have turned into pneumonia but hadn't and more. This wise, old woman is how I prefer to think of myself. But in my unconscious denial of the shadow side of growing older, I had become brittle, reactive, controlling. And what's more, I didn't realize I was doing any of this—and certainly not that it might have anything to do with turning 70.

Finally, I took my complaints to my dear friend Connie, older, wiser, and fiercer than I. She listened patiently. Took a deep breath and replied: "You're attempting to pour concrete on your life—to freeze who you once were so as not to let it erode any further; to protect yourself and those for whom you care from the uncertainties of the future. But no pushing through, battling, or overcoming will stop time. Instead, why not try opening up empty space into which you can be free to flow? Then let yourself be open to whatever unfolds, giving yourself permission to accept the whole of life as it arises, sometimes sad, sometimes joyful, sometimes flat out astonishing!"

My friend said more, but I had begun quietly weeping as my revivified heart cracked open, shattering the concrete into little pieces. And there I sat, reduced to a puddle of love. And here I remain, having made it through to the other side of my milestone birthday, floating along on tears of humility and gratitude.

If one is fortunate to endure long enough, that which we resist mysteriously transforms into something one no longer hopes to escape. Rather, one becomes willing to embrace the whole of it with a deep, quiet understanding of the bittersweet nature of life. Letting go of what once was or might never be or of what still is no matter how hard we try to make an improvement is no longer a punishment, but a place so true and so deep, it can't be spoken.

THE SENSES

I pick up a book and attempt to read but my intellect refuses to engage. It is not that I'm bored or tired—but that so many words gathered in one place have come to feel like a seduction. They lure me upwards into my mind, when it is my body that beckons to me for attention. I did not expect to find myself to be a sensualist at my age. But in the truest sense of the word—scent, sight, taste, hearing, and touch—I am more keenly honed than ever.

The rough feel of the damask on my deck chair where I write—the firm give of the cushion. These fill me with delight and I do not prefer that reading—or writing—be allowed to distract me from it. Rather, it is as if I had never before sipped lavender tea, draped myself in such a soft blanket. My bed is warm in the winter. Cool in the summer. How could this be? This new sensuality—this embodiment of pleasure—is so far the saving grace of older age. It compensates for the losses, if not entirely, at least a fair amount.

I used to be restless, ambitious, acquisitive. When there were prizes to be awarded, banquets, fireworks, I wanted to be there. Didn't want to miss out. However, I already know these things. I've already had plenty. But to sit quietly enjoying the smooth feel of the yellow pad in my hands: I am in no hurry to write.

THREE OCTOGENARIANS

Three women, octogenarians, sit side by side at open windows. Behind each are institutionalized bustle and the faint scent of antiseptic. Outside, there are trees and a garden and a light spring breeze. Each sits perfectly still and any differences between them are not apparent. But one has achieved something wonderful. She is content.

Not the first, who is upset that she has had no visitors this week. She has let go of hope, certain that she has been abandoned and doomed to a slow, lonely death. For the second, the pain of living is a thing of the past. No one has visited her, either. She has also let go, not only of hope, but of everything. Beyond sadness, anger, and fear, she has fallen asleep with her eyes open. She is waiting to die, her only concern being that it may not come soon enough.

The third has also let go—but she is the one who is content. Beyond the demands of the life she has left behind, she has discovered the pure joy of simple pleasure. She is the only one of the three who notices the leaves as they dance in the wind. She is fascinated by the movements of shade and shadow. When a bird alights, when a squirrel bounds, she gasps with delight. She understands that letting go is not the same as giving up, in or out. It is, rather, the ability to transcend faltering expectations to see the good that remains: to allow the shadows to be without taking the light for granted.

Others may not care or understand. No matter. She is beyond submitting that which matters most to the judgment of others. No need to explain, defend or excuse. How brightly her eyes do shine!

Aging is a time full of irony. We find ourselves brimming with unexpected passion, but frequently lack the energy to see things through.

We experience ourselves to be at the peak of our knowledge and abilities, only to realize that we are masters of a world that no longer exists.

At times we are full of purpose; other times we wonder what it has all been for.

We did not anticipate facing a new threshold this late in life, feeling more alive than ever.

The irony nearly breaks us, as we leapfrog through the mystery of age one paradox at a time.

II
LEGACY OF BEING

Anticipated regret and unexpected passion

IN THE GAP

We who are older, wiser, fiercer have moments when we experience ourselves to be merged with the divine—where we know we are capable of acting in concord with God's will for us. In the moment, we know we are good and that life is inherently meaningful. But it doesn't stick. It's easier when we are in the grip of suffering to cry out for mercy and accept God's gracious embrace. But when things are even one click short of annihilation, life drags us back into the mundane.

I only experience moments of unity sometimes, but I experience the yearning for merger most of the time and in the gap is where I find myself living much of my life. How does one reconcile one's experience and one's aspirations? Perhaps the answer is hidden in plain sight. For it is in the gap that creativity arises. In the breach is where we aspire, we explore, we redeem, we experiment, we practice, and we build. There are times, too, when all we can do is persist, but this also implies some lure drawing us forward toward hope, however dimly felt.

A VISION

When we come into age, we aspire to be serene, but it's complicated. At any given time, we may set our gears to neutral, allowing gravity to have its way with us as we gather speed on the down ramp to mortality. Then we have second thoughts, shifting full throttle into reverse. If we thought to not only slow the descent but to roar back into the life we left behind, we may be disappointed that we are not tearing it up—but puttering. No wonder our engines give out.

I write this from first-hand experience, several weeks after an incident that landed me in the emergency room. The day of the incident started like many others—but, of course, every day I am a little older, a little changed. On this particular day, family came for brunch. We managed to prepare and serve the meal, all while keeping the two youngest and three dogs—busy and safe.

Afterwards, I settled into the sofa—the only still spot in a house full of moving parts—when suddenly a bolt of light coming through the window struck my eyes. While it was storming outside, this was no flash of lightning, but the beginning of a hallucination: timeless space in which a shimmering cosmic egg radiated beams of light. Dan entered my field of vision in fractal echoes of himself, like the cubist depiction of a nude descending a staircase. I tried to describe what was happening in my best story-telling voice, not wanting to disturb the children. At his insistence, we headed to the ER to be evaluated for a stroke.

If I had been in my right mind, I would have been dismayed by the rapidity with which I was reduced from a woman on full throttle to an institutionalized unit on the medical production line. But I wasn't in my right mind—and perhaps I have rarely been so. Rather, encased in my default mind, I decided to not only make the best of this, but to put on a show. I would be the happiest, funniest person ever to submit to intensive care. I would be the most popular patient in history, cracking jokes on the gurney en route to various examinations. Then they would let me live.

Even before the tests began, the vision had already faded and now, weeks after the ER incident, I have had the last of a string of good news. No sign of stroke: only a transitory ocular migraine. Bothersome but nothing serious. And if I weren't going to die from it, I might yet have died of mortification for having been such a bother.

Everybody says I did the smart thing checking it out, but it is so hard for me to stop worrying about how I could have allowed myself to be a burden to others, the thought never crossing my mind that when you're in intensive care, you are in the ultimate setting to receive care—intensively.

It may look like weakness, asking for help. But what is really going on is that I am now determined to stop performing for others not as a withdrawal from life, but because I am so passionate about it. I am grateful for this experience for allowing me to recognize that being at the mercy of forced exuberance is no different than giving one encore too many.

THE HAPPY GHOST

Not long ago, after recovering from the flu, there was a happy ghost wandering through the hallways of our little cottage on the river. She paused at a handmade miniature house made from clay, remembering when her son had gifted her with it years ago. There was her special collection of teas and shelf full of books she had loved. She passed her hand over the colorful antique knit throw on the sofa—what a find that had been. The happy ghost chuckled over the secret the draped throw so artfully kept: a corner of the couch nibbled bare by one of the dogs when she was just a pup. As the ghost meandered, she sighed in wonderment at what she had made of her life: nothing fancy–no mansion, no fame. But at the same time, so much more than she'd ever dared hope for: the sense of having fulfilled what she had come here to do. Then, turning the corner, the happy ghost stubbed her toe and remembered that she was still here, embodied: felt her life come throbbing back into her from the sole up. And could not help but ask the question: "Walking around my house weeping for joy as if I had already passed . . . Is this normal?"

Perhaps on top of my own brush with mortality, I've experienced one death too many recently. A number seem to have slipped away while I was looking the other direction. The blustery professor who once held sway over so many receding into the shadows of an assisted living facility with nary a whisper to mark his final passage. A t'ai chi instructor admitted to hospice, only his inner circle in attendance to witness his decline. The dramatic narratives of their lives had ceased demanding our attention, quieting down but not over: the distillation of their lives still radiating each particular and unique essence through the sheer conjuring of a name.

Becoming one's self is not as easy as it seems—although these two and so many more who are gone but not forgotten, made it look effortless. Each released the domination of their egos—whether by choice or by circumstance—merging into the flow of life. This is something one begins to practice every time one intuits that it no longer matters whether one is radiating one's essence center stage or in an intimate salon; every time one savors the present moment in a pause, so redolent, so embracing of all of life, that the veil between ourselves and Presence dissipates. What was once impenetrable now seems as delicate and precious as gossamer.

So that was what the happy ghost was doing in my house: practicing. Having loosened the grip on so much of what I used to believe defined me, and yet something remains: the silken threads of my final attachments—that which has taken a lifetime to realize is most precious. Attachment to what? A ceramic model? A cup of tea? A nibbled couch? No, not the things themselves. Neither the pause nor even the promise of what is yet to come. But rather: how good it is to be alive.

THE FACTS OF LIFE

For once, or perhaps finally, the facts of my life seem beside the point. Yes, the disagreement with a good friend that consumed most of a week turned out to be a simple miscommunication. But one hard-won act of reclamation cannot alone compensate for all the losses that just yesterday bedeviled me. Objectively, whole worlds of connection continue to be lost: work, friendship, public platforms.

So how is it possible that today, every resentment, every jealousy, every regret seems unwarranted? Every transgression forgiven? Today, I sit here in this new, wholly unexpected place, wishing everybody well. It is as though everything that has happened to me—not just recently, but since the jolt of my first breath—has been in service of something. Like sandpaper: the abrasion of life has effected the removal of all but the essential. Every fact on the list—the chaos, the rejection, the wounding: grains of sand that scrape and file to reveal the smoothed contours of what had been hidden, waiting to be revealed.

This shift, which seems so sudden today but has taken the whole of my life, requires not a single adjustment of history or biography to finally deliver long sought-after joy. This glimpse of essence is beyond the facts of anything of our world, and certainly beyond anything of my doing. The facts of my life: revealed, glorious and more or less irrelevant.

GARBED IN HOLINESS

Even toward the end of her life, my mother and I still didn't agree on a whole lot. For example, I would have preferred she convince Dad to keep their downtown condo with the awesome view, but they opted for a gated adult community in the suburbs. So okay. Their choice. But one thing Mom and I shared was disapproval of my father's wardrobe.

All his life, Dad opted for comfort. During the day, he dressed the part of your old-school family physician complete with nifty bow tie. But as soon as he hit the front porch, he never changed into anything that wouldn't have been soft enough to sleep in. He donned hand-knit sweaters and polyester pantsuits way before they were trendy.

But this was not what caused Mom and me distress. Once he retired, his wardrobe ossified. No new items were ever installed—at least not out of free will. Rather, his collection of favorites was left to fend for itself. The hand-knit sweaters got softer still as they aged, worn literally to the nub. When his favorite pair of polyester running pants sprouted a hole, Mom and I tricked him into a changing room at a Sears where while trying on new bottoms, the old ones were quietly spirited away never to be seen again.

I have to say that in the end, the holes won. No matter how much and often we cajoled, implored and connived, the holes popped up faster and more persistently. Dad, who in this regard felt blessed to be hard of hearing, died at 91 a happy man.

So here I am, in my mere seventies, with not only another confession—but a revelation. My wardrobe: it's full of holes. And what's more, I don't intend to do anything about it. I get it, Dad. I understand the absolute joy of discovering a button down that embraces you with comfort. A pullover so soft and light it is as if joy itself were kissing your body.

These didn't become favorites by accident—and they are irreplaceable. The hand-loomed sweater bought in Ireland, the only one at the mill—probably in the whole world—with cashmere woven into the blend. When will I ever get back to Ireland—traveling with my adult daughter on a European road trip—stumbling onto the mill—finding this one perfect sweater in the world? The very same sweater that Molly, the poodle/Shih-Tzu mix, recently nibbled a hole into.

Then there's my other favorite—this one an airy mohair woven from yarn so light it could almost float away. I know only I could love this because it was the very last sweater on the mark-down rack of what had been my favorite clothing store's closing sale, plummeting down from the stratospheres I could never afford to a cool $15 because who, besides me, in their right mind would want to wear a giant frothy pink skull across her chest? I love this sweater so much, I have come to think of it as my spirit animal. The Irish sweater will get a patch so as to prevent further unraveling. But the skull mohair now has holes not only on the front, but all over the place, impossible to repair but beloved nevertheless.

Neither my husband nor my children have said anything to me about any of this yet. But then again, not only are they better people than I—but apparently clothes with holes in them have become fashionable. Still, I have to make peace with this for myself—the aging of not only my wardrobe, but of myself. When I was younger, my closet—like my life—was a river, raging with purpose. Clothing that manifested holes were let go of easily and replaced with something better. Now my closet—and my life—are more like a pond: quieted down, contained. Everything in it has become that much more precious because it cannot or will not be replaced.

And there you have it: It was I who threw Dad's pants away into the Sears' garbage while he stood just behind the curtain trapped helpless in his boxers. I get it now, Dad. You not only wore your holes—you

CAROL ORSBORN, PH.D.

cherished them. It was never about suffering a deficit of self-respect. I see now that your level of self-respect was just fine, and that in addition you had achieved a level of freedom to which I now aspire. Stripped of false ego and illusion, the veil between you and the Divine had worn thin, indeed. Worn to the nub, in fact.

CONFESSION

I confess to my shortcomings. In fact, in the still hours before dawn, confession is what comes easiest to me. But when I tell the whole truth about myself, I must admit to the good things, too. This does not take place in a flash of recognition, but by grindingly slow evolution.

It has taken many years to make some improvement, doing whatever I can to leave our children and future generations a legacy of love and righteousness. But in order to do this, I have had to surrender the notion that I am God's appointed helper, imbued with special powers. It was well-meaning: my desire to save those for whom I care from pain, to fix wrongs that were not my doing and to intervene in choices that were not my business. At last, I've reached a point where I can truly celebrate that my legacy is not only the love that inspired my hopes for them, but the honesty, humility and acceptance I am practicing one apology, one act of forgiveness, one expression of compassion at a time.

I now know that the culmination of this long journey is not achievement—but appreciation. Sometimes, this is bittersweet: an appreciation of the limits of the human condition. There will always be challenges encountered and attempts made to overcome—sometimes succeeding, sometimes not. Sometimes, I grieve that life has to be this hard. Other times, I am simply and quietly in awe of what could be something small—and sometimes of it all. Where I was once hard-charging, certain of the need for extraordinary effort, I can now be tender and receptive. I can feel sad without feeling weak; I can feel anger and know it to be justified; I can forgive myself and others and be grateful for this grand journey we are on together.

Recognizing this—and even a small advance will do—I am clear that my life makes sense: that I have come to fulfill some higher purpose. When I touch such moments, all the rest—the missteps, transgressions, failings—are no longer front and center. Rather, they take their place beside my gifts and I embrace the whole of life, delighted with my part in it.

How does one reconcile one's experience and one's aspirations? After all these years, striving to leave a legacy of love . . . and still I persist.

Perhaps the answer is hidden in plain sight. For it is only in the gap that the urge to do better arises. In the breech, too, there is faith and mercy.

In the end, we find that the only path to realization was never a leap, but stepping stones: hobbling our way toward a legacy one apology, one moment of forgiveness, one expression of compassion at a time.

III
OUR TIMES
The state of the world in our culminating moment

JAWS AGAPE

Born in the ebullient wake of World War II, our generation largely bought into the narrative that our country was a beacon of light standing up to evil, and that goodness had and would always in the end prevail. I confess that I so believed in our cohort's commitment to love and justice, I was sure that zeitgeist would do the heavy lifting for us. Not anymore. My misguided faith in the trajectory of history has at last grown teeth. Words are being voiced that should have been spoken years ago. Habits that once offered comfortable places to hide are being confronted and smashed. Inconvenient emotions and intuitions are being heeded. I see the misplaced faith that has stuck to my feet like tar in sand, and am going to great lengths in an attempt to walk it away. This work of reclamation is as critical as it is painful. And there are no guarantees that I will succeed in this lifetime.

We humans are so gifted with potential: opposable thumbs, frontal lobes, consciousness itself. With these, we can imagine, dream, build, create. But these assets show us not only that of which we are capable, but how often our potential for manifesting greatness is dashed. Oh dear ones, how much of our gifts do we waste on pursuits and concerns not worthy of us? Why is it so hard to be magnificent?

There is plenty of guilt, shame and regret to go around. But if we stop confusing wallowing with introspection, we can appropriate our vital energy and invest it into setting things right. But will this transpire in our lifetime? Our hard-won humility hints otherwise. We meant to leave a legacy that would inspire. Instead, we leave a warning.

NOT TOO LATE

When it comes to our differences, we aim to be the bigger person. But why do so many people have to be asleep, stupid, selfish, and just plain bad?

How can so many have become confused about something as basic as right versus wrong? For many, the line between truth and lies has become blurred. There are those at all poles of the spectrum who would manipulate us by fostering fear and offering safety only within one's own tribe. Along the way, the urge to pick a side to establish something akin to everyday life had been heeded, shared illusions unconsciously adopted, if we were to get on with it.

Societal forces have and continue to conspire to rock us into a somnambulistic half-life.

We have taken many things for granted, not the least of which is the durability of the legacy we thought we were leaving future generations. We didn't expect this late in life to find ourselves living in a new world, without a map. Many of us are sad, scared, confused, angry, ashamed. It is discomforting, indeed, to confront the shadows not only in others, but in one's self, to be awakened only to discover that to live one's truth, one may be doomed to feeling wretched much of the time.

Perhaps if we were less connected, we would not have to cringe so often. But what alternative do we have when every time we turn on our computers and phones, every time we pass a television or electronic billboard, we are faced with the shadow of humanity?

It is not easy to be old in these difficult times, wishing one had done, could, or can do more. Still, it is not too late to tell the truth. Not too late to have compassion for the generations who will live with the ramifications of our shortcomings. Not too late to change what we can. And finally, not too late to have compassion for ourselves given that however much we do, it won't be enough.

REAR-VIEW MIRROR

Our generation of older women put our lives and careers on the line to open doors for our daughters. We had hoped it would have been easier for them than it has turned out to be. We underestimated that, all the while, we had been connected to primal archetypes running like a deep underground river beneath our daily lives.

Much of the tension of the world can be reduced to the battle between the feminine versus the masculine. Embodied in male energy is the urge to compete and the will to impose order while female energy nurtures and unites. Women hold the capacity to soften the harsher edges, to influence and to midwife rejuvenation on those occasions when the masculine, left to its own devices, bludgeons others and himself into a stupor. But as soon as he catches his breath—be it days or decades—the masculine archetype is back at it again. Fearing that in the interim too much power may have been granted his helpmate, he quells her power, uses his strength to relegate her to the shadows. And there she stayed, cooking, cleaning, tending the children, and alternately denying, deflecting and, when possible, exploiting his secret weaknesses.

But the times we live in are different. This time, when male-dominated forces came home from their various wars, many women refused to collude with belittlement. Women's rights, gender equality: in a society that is still so overtly masculinized, where misogyny can still sway elections, it is easy to forget how far we've come. Younger women can take advantage of new opportunities—freedoms in relating to the world both in and outside the home. But they do so in a society that largely continues to view women through a rear-view mirror. Liberation for them has often meant the right to struggle privately, persist courageously, protest publicly. But how gratifying it is to witness so many taking action, demanding a place at the table.

But why is it taking so long? In our final season, we are called to become conscious of the truth that not only have we had to struggle with forces larger than ourselves, but that it would be up to a new generation of women to help us realize that we, too, have always been more than we had thought ourselves to be. Ultimately, if we live the gift of age deep and full, we come to realize that the tension of the archetype of male versus female is not a thing to resolve, conquer or transcend—but to reap.

LOCK-STEP

The urge to challenge the status quo is the most precious of human impulses. How sad that there has been so much resistance to putting the necessary investment into young people's education so that they learn to do so intelligently. History, the arts, literature and the social sciences must be taught for the purpose of discernment and self-knowledge. Without these, we create a population easy to manipulate even against its own interests. Over time the young can grow into adulthood alienated from their own hearts and minds.

Mercifully, this lock-step walk in group unconsciousness is not universal. There are individuals who hail from all the generations who not only resist the efforts that conspire to put us to sleep, but intensely oppose it. There are many who stand for compassion and justice, who take risks and are willing to tell the truth even when doing so puts them in danger. Among these are many—but not all—of the old, who benefited from the lessons of the past, for whom a robust education was a priority, whose love for their offspring and concern for the future has evoked fresh courage and the will to act.

The contrast between those who follow and those who resist is so stark that while the pervasive atmosphere we live in is darkness, never have the stars been brighter, more able to point the way. There is no room for complacency, and so there can be no room for hopelessness.

ADVANCES

Technology. Genetic engineering. Food modification. Scientific advances impacting every field of endeavor. Most of us don't like many of the changes that are taking place in the name of progress. The urge is great to withdraw. But if we do so, do we collude in marginalizing and silencing ourselves at a time when our world needs us more than ever?

My mystical friends say it's all an illusion anyway, and some of them have succeeded in severing ties to what they view as a corrupted world. But have they merely traded moral fervor for complacency? Confused transcendence with denial? Don't we have a responsibility to stay engaged even if only to protest?

The world is moving forward into the future, whether we like it or not. Our new generation of elders has lived the changes every day, year after year. Over the span of our long lives, we've had to make difficult choices over and over again, to rise to whatever occasion life brings our way, or shrink away: to hide or refuse. To choose to stay engaged inevitably entails risk. And growth has been a risk many of us have always been willing to take.

So here's the heart of it. While we are not as in control of as much as we wished we were, we are called to use whatever influence we have in us for the greater good. Of course, staying engaged opens up the possibility of making less than perfect decisions, but then again, we are all imperfect people living in an imperfect world.

And so it is that this imperfect person living in imperfect times hopes to do what I can to make the world and myself better than we otherwise would have been.

HUMAN POTENTIAL

Our generation accepted the imperative to fulfill one's human potential. But we misunderstood. The human potential is not limited to the thin slice of the spectrum we tend to think of as happiness or of peace. To be fully alive, we must avail ourselves of the entire range, including bittersweet sorrow, righteous indignation, and grief. Add but these few shadows, and there is suddenly some texture, some depth some softening to the truth to our lives.

But then again, these are not the entire spectrum. What of vindictiveness, cunning, complacency, rage and violence? When I was younger, I could more easily distract myself from aspects of humanity I was unwilling to grant attention. Now, with unassigned time on my hands, I am less protected from knowledge of the cruelties that people inflict upon one another, less able to hide from my own shadows, less likely to speak about the fulfillment of the human potential, as if in doing so I could somehow get it all to turn out the way I'd like.

Now that I am old, I discover I have a new potential—one that I would never have thought myself willing to embrace. To deplore. Deplore is the right word—a much better word than recoil. Deplore dives through hardened crusts of avoidance and complacency, busting through to the very heart of things. Deplore opens up jagged cracks and gaping holes. Pain gets through, somehow feeling very much like love. And like love, you know you have truly reached the limit of your own human potential when you can bear no more.

WHITEWASH

I was raised to believe that sadness is wallowing, anger uncalled for, and fear self-indulgent. In its place, we picked ourselves up by our bootstraps and marched ourselves to the front lines every day in every way, in command and in control. At the same time, I always carried the suspicion that there could be something more to life begging to be revealed, if only I knew where to look. I did not think to dive into the darkness. Rather, it felt organic—natural even—to go with my gut. And my gut told me, more often than not: "Run!"

But negative emotions denied do not just go away, they grow secret roots that penetrate every thought and emotion, entwining one's heart with tendrils of doubt. It turns out that the very effort one exerts to suppress, manage, or eliminate negativity becomes part of the shadow, itself. Our attempts to love unconditionally, forced to bend around unacknowledged envy, betrayal, and disappointment, become gnarly. Without boundaries, accommodating can be martyrdom walking hand in hand with passive aggression. Eventually, we have done everything we can think of to be the light, and yet the shadows persist.

That's when we realize that we have no choice but to come to terms with our shadow. To become whole, we would seek to acknowledge, understand, and embrace what we previously rejected about ourselves—but hold it lightly, tenderly with compassion for oneself, and for the human condition. This sounds good. And may even work sometimes, even for extended periods. But the shadow, ultimately, demands something more of us than peace. The shadow demands authenticity.

To accept one's own authenticity, one does not simply love away one's sadness and anger. One becomes whole when one tells the truth about whatever emotion has taken hold. When we truly accept anger, we are not peaceful. We are angry. When we accept sadness, we are not joyful, we are sad. Only then does a shift become possible. But if a shift is to come, it won't be of our own doing.

For those of us who invested so much energy in achieving mastery, this is, indeed, an ordeal. To feel whatever has risen to the surface for you with no need to understand it? No need, even, for naming? No second-guessing; no peace-making or appeasement; no story about where it came from, what it means or what one needs to do about it? One neither clings nor lets go. The feeling is free to linger, or dig in, to shift about or move on. One is no more tempted to manage its journey than to make demands of the clouds as they pass overhead.

But even this degree of surrender bears no guarantees, for this is not a transaction. It is, rather, an act of blind faith; and if the shadows do lift, this is the gift of mercy and of grace.

I now realize that, in fact, it was never my job to embrace anything, either the shadow or the light. Rather, it is God who embraces me.

It is not easy to be old in these times, wishing one had done or could do more. We aim to be the bigger person, but why do so many people have to be asleep, stupid, selfish and just plain bad?

The call is to make a sincere attempt to find common ground with those who we find disagreeable. But this has nothing to do with becoming the bigger person.

Rather, what is called for is humility. To discern the difference between being powerful and being called. And if one is not yet sure, we must at least not cover up the tension we cannot deny while preparing to respond.

IV
THE PARADOX OF
RELATEDNESS

*The tension between wanting to
belong and the desire for solitude*

THE RISK

At first, it is a shock to be marginalized from others' lives, to discover that our children have grown up to live on their own and that society has somehow gone on, for better or worse, without us in the lead. Later, it comes as another jolt to realize those times when we may no longer need—or want—the distraction relationship entails. We actively seek solitude, enjoy our own company, and can't be bothered with small talk or entanglements. Invariably, interactions with others deplete or at least complicate our lives. The intensity of relatedness we once craved—that defined us—becomes a burden to be shed. Oh, we can keep the relationships going, if we like. But dear God, please not the drama.

There is freedom in this and joy as the distinct contours of one's inner terrain become revealed, begging to be explored and enjoyed. We surprise ourselves every day, experiencing an intimacy of relatedness to our de-peopled world beyond anything previously known. But is it possible to go too far? One believes one is choosing freedom, but when the phone stops ringing, emails slow down, visits become special events rather than part of one's routine? Is this a slippery slope leading not to solitude—intimacy with one's inner life and with God—but to loneliness? Separation from God?

When one is young, there is no second-guessing the urge for solitude. One closes the door to refresh oneself but the baby cries and it's back to the fray. But when there is no cry to call you back, does sinking into solitude serve as an end in itself? Or is one somehow not only missing something important, but the point? Perhaps both are true—another paradox of age. But I have at least the beginning of an answer. For those of us who have overinvested in years of busyness, productivity, and noise, better to meet this core question—this tension—in silence, at least until the angst quiets and certainty emerges spontaneously.

This is the risk that age demands we take: to believe that our deepest, quietest urge for connection to God can be trusted. If one is meant to return to the active life, it can be God's cry, not a baby's, that will summon us. And if we return, out of quiet rather than agitation, we do not leave what we have discovered of ourselves behind. Rather, we bring our deepened relationship to ourselves, to life and to God with us.

DO NOT DISTURB

We who are old yearn to be authentic—isn't this the least we've earned from our many long years: our hard-won right to express our unvarnished truth? But then, how to be both honest and yet not disturb others when asked "How are you feeling?" Don't we, at a minimum, have the right to tell the honest truth about whatever is going on with us? But others— especially the young—are consumed with troubles of their own, and merely want to know that we are at least alright enough for them to get back to their own pressing concerns.

If we are to be gracious, we leave things out. We make an attempt to play the part of the better self we aspire to be. But to feign cheeriness, even though it satisfies others, also feels like a betrayal of self.

Why does it matter so much to us, this excess of self that can find no place in polite conversation? Is it possible we are so foolish as to believe that what has befallen us could otherwise serve as some kind of lesson to others? Is it the ego that wishes to make one's maladies known, earning admiration for one's strength and fortitude? And even if we choose not to play the victim and keep our issues a secret, is this merely to demonstrate to ourselves what heroism, what sacrifice, what discipline!

The urge to be truly heard and understood is powerful. Can we mere humans hope to transcend this entitlement while breath is still ours? If we aim for spiritual perfection, we might as well call it a day. But find that fine line between self-betrayal and flooding others with too much of ourselves and there one can find some at least temporary release in a newly acquired aptitude for courtesy.

GESTATION

All my many years, it was only during the course of my pregnancies that I had an experience of not being the center of my life. So many years invested—before and after—working to establish my value, to make a name for myself. But over the course of those 9 months, I shared my lungs, my blood and my heart in order to gestate new life. While it was completely different than anything else I'd ever known, I grew used to it—came to enjoy the freedom of selflessness, knowing that all I had to do to make meaning of life was simply to be.

How ironic that now that I am old—after all these years striving to be Someone—I am once again not the point. These days, I go to open a can and it defies me, waiting for someone else to do the job. A loved one's knee is bruised, and other lips get there before mine. I reach out to my most recent editor only to be greeted by a new, young voice who doesn't know who I am or where she went. You see it on the news, at the gym, in the subway: an entire generation of offspring grows stronger and stronger with every kick.

It is as if old age were the last month of a lifelong gestation. There is barely enough room for us in life, our very bodies having become something impersonal: an institutionalized carrier of a future that will not be ours.

And yet, once again, I am growing used to it— enjoying the freedom of knowing anew that all I have to do to justify my existence is simply to be.

BREATHING SPACE

We have learned things that could benefit others. But growing into age teaches us that lives never look to those peeking in the same as how it feels to be living out one's own destiny. From the outside, most of us look if not broken at least bent. But from within, there exists the opportunity to make sense of things.

We become older, wiser, and fiercer when we grow large enough to simultaneously embrace both the imperfection and the grace of the human condition with compassion and kindness for other and for self. What a blessing when we discover that we have the capacity to respect others even when they fall short of our expectations; that we can persist in loving even when we are misunderstood; that we can engage bravely even knowing that despite the best of intentions, we are bound to disappoint one another from time to time; and above all, that we can be gifted with a bittersweet poignancy that makes the letting go bearable.

Life moves on, sometimes lurching, sometimes faltering. But invariably, under brush, in a cave, nestled in a tree knot, something new is taking its first breath.

MULCH

The problem with intimacy between a man and a woman is also its grace, especially when it comes to those long marriages that not only endure, but thrive. In the early days, we court and marry our ideal. If the basics are in place—attraction, affinity, viability—we can overlook much that may not have been on the original checklist. But we hide at least some of our own shortcomings, as well.

Few make it past the honeymoon before discrepancies crop up. Even in the best of marriages, it doesn't take long to realize that the public persona that operates seamlessly on the world stage collapses when the curtain falls. In the behind-the-scenes intimacy of marriage, we see our mates' weaknesses and foibles, vulnerabilities and worse. If the marriage is to deepen, we do not run—we come closer. We see one another naked and exposed, and love anyway. This is mercy. This is grace. And this, too, is the best case scenario.

If the marriage is to send its roots deep enough to withstand the challenges of a long life together, we must literally grow together through time. But growth is, at its heart, a messy, complicated affair. Of course, we grow closer through the good times, when we reap the results of good decisions and share both hoped-for and unexpected good fortune. We find it easy to be generous, kind, loving when the sun is shining and a warm breeze carries us along side by side to fertile ground. But we also grow in the midst of the muddied soil of disillusionment, if we are brave or fool-hearty enough to stay rather than flee, accepting that our vows were meant to be an aspiration, not an incantation. It all turns to fertile mulch—the disappointment with our loved one, with ourselves, and with life—if we let it. We grow through repressing anger, expressing it, and making up. We grow through tendering forgiveness even or especially when we know it was the other who was in the wrong. And we grow through offering forgiveness to ourselves, too.

Over time, we have bumped into, bruised, exposed, and explored every shadowy crevice we had once hoped to keep well-hid from one another, the things we are sure make us unlovable. And when we stay, return, or allow ourselves to be found, over and over again, we discover a love larger than ourselves. This is why marriage is a sacrament for, at its best, it holds the potential not only to unite us with one another, but with God.

A GLORIOUS END

While we may at least theoretically have some say over whom and how many we love, we have absolutely no control over who loves us. You may well wish someone in particular would make you the object of their affection—show yourself to be worthy, deserving, attractive enough to merit favored status, and of course you are. In fact, it would take a fool to overlook your many obvious qualities.

The thing is, there is no shortage of fools. It takes many, many years to finally come to realize that who and how many decide to love you has nothing at all to do with your worth. The learning curve is steep, and one pays perhaps too great a price in extinguishing the need for love to come from any particular source, which is always easier said than done.

But people do break addictions. They clutch the sides of their beds in hot and cold shivers, crying out for help from the depths of despair. And just when all seems lost comes a glimmer of light bearing the obvious truth. Failed love does indeed burn—but it burns away only that which was never really yours. I would expect at the end of the transmutation to be resigned, complacent. Some call this suffering but it is also ecstasy. For in the end, what remains is both fierce and glorious.

CALLED TO STRUGGLE

When I was young, I perceived the biggest threats to meaning as coming from outside myself. I was concerned with survival and needed God's support to help me endure the otherwise unbearable. But with age new threats arise and God is no longer the One who saves me from the struggle. In fact, I now experience God as the One calling me to struggle.

On a good day, I see this as growth. On these days, I feel myself answering God's call toward psychological and spiritual maturity, consenting to engage with my shadows, not just once, but for as long as necessary. But when the weather turns and the storm clouds crowd in, I can forget everything. On these days, I pity myself, asking why I have come this far—have made so many amends—only to be experiencing aspects of myself I had thought to have laid to rest long ago? Nevertheless, sooner or later, and often despite myself, I take them on. But does it really have to be so hard?

I would welcome a once and for all transcendence or conversion—God knows I'm willing—but instead find myself having to make the choice to be my better self, decision by decision. When the occasion calls for it, and I remember, I choose to be patient rather than impetuous. I choose to face my fears and flaws and struggle if not with, at least toward hope. It's not easy, I don't always succeed, and even when I do, it doesn't always take.

I am embarrassed by the very notion of becoming a partner with God in this, even if only to wrestle. How audacious! I can do this if I don't think—just do it—but seeing the words written down gives me serious pause. Yet God is here, even in the pause, whispering to me. "Yes, dear one. Even you."

A NEW SEASON

Lucky has finally submitted to the seasonal indignity of donning her red down dog coat. We'd thought that when the temperatures plummeted the squirrels would disappear and she would lose interest in running outside. But while it is true there isn't the frantic activity that accompanied late fall, the bared branches have revealed the secret pathways of the hardiest of the squirrels Lucky's terrier breed was bred to chase.

All twelve years of her long life: chasing squirrels through all the seasons. Lush summer days, the squirrels hidden amongst the thick leaves, only visible on mad dashes. Fall and spring: frantic running, jumping, scrambling, playing tag in circles around tree trunks. In the deep freeze of winter, Lucky hand-carried home from the yard against her will before she catches cold. Re-installed on her warm perch at the window only to start the game all over again. A blast of excited barks: "Let me out now, now, now!" Her two furry step-siblings, Molly and Sammy, not so interested in squirrels, but not wanting to miss any opportunity to cut loose. And all of us curious but not too worried about it. What would Lucky do with a squirrel if she ever did catch one? Season after season. Year after year. Always nearly, almost, just missed, not quite.

Then this fall, we found out. Lucky leading the pack out to the farthest tree and even faster back to the front stoop, all three of them bursting with excited agitation. In her mouth, held gently as a pup, a baby squirrel. Understandably rattled, the squirrel looked squarely at me with unblinking eyes. Okay, I screamed a little. But nevertheless, I produced a towel, accepting the tiny, quivering body as the gift he was intended to be, whisking him to safety where after a breathless moment of stunned silence the tiny creature scampered gracefully away. Oh life, oh squirrel life, oh dog life, oh my life.

Since then, things are different. Lucky still sits in the window watching diligently. When she spots a squirrel, she still barks like crazy, begging to be let out. Wrapped in down, she still runs as fast as her little legs will carry her. Now, in her well-seasoned years, with just a touch of arthritis in her knees, perhaps not so fast as before, but fast enough. And then she just sits down and watches.

Emboldened, the handful of intrepid deep winter squirrels now scamper freely around her, leaping from one fully exposed bare branch to another, right above her cold, wet upturned nose. But Lucky no longer chases squirrels.

She loves them.

We who have endured the most decades have had the opportunity to witness patterns of loving and wounding, ambition and disappointment, advance and setback cycling through time on well-worn tracks.

Never have we had more to share, and never have we felt more marginalized. We struggle with our wanting to belong—and the desire for solitude.

Paradoxically, it is on the margins that we develop new capacities to not only experience our greatest love, but to discover that we are beloved.

V
DEFEAT AND VICTORY
What is lost, what is gained through aging

CANDIDATES

When I speak to others about things that really matter, certain eyes shine brighter than others. These are the ones who have endured more than their fair share of difficulties. They are recovering alcoholics, divorcees, or parents who have buried a child. They have suffered deprivation and illness. They have been forced to admit that they are not in control. And as it turns out, it is the things we fear most that carry the capacity to become catalysts for what we most value: the deepest appreciation of life, the unspeakable grace of a heart broken open.

When we allow hardship and suffering to do their work over time, the ripened spirit bursts forth to inhabit one's naturally abundant world. One realizes at last how little rather than how much one truly needs to be fulfilled. One needs fewer engagements, opportunities, even other people. One can finally stop and simply take one deep, satisfying breath after another. One feels oneself no longer to be who one used to be—not even Somebody—discovering that this is perfectly fine. The experience of the more that we pursued turns out to be right here, right now with nothing else one must do or be.

But suffering is neither a guarantee nor a prescription for fulfillment. Even the losses associated with aging may not result in the spiritual ripening and psychological maturity to which we aspire. In fact, one is just as likely to become hard and bitter—one's soul shriveling up like a withered apple—should one refuse the invitation hardship issues to become vulnerable rather than redouble efforts to bolster reinforcement. But some degree of suffering does seem to be a prerequisite for transformation.

And since suffering comes to us all, we are all candidates.

A TENDER SHOOT

Asking for mercy is a brave act, for one must first admit that one has done wrong and is, devoid of intervention, helpless to do anything more about it. And while if being granted mercy does ameliorate the pain of the shortcoming, it doesn't erase everything. We live into the future, neither cleansed nor forgetful, but with both the mercy and the thing that necessitated it. In this way, mercy is better—if less desired—than purification because we are forced to live with the humanity of our imperfection.

Nobody forgets anything. In fact, we remember how much unhappiness we have experienced and inflicted. Some of it may have been intended—but much of it is the collateral damage that takes place at the dangerous crossroads between past and present as a by-product of the organic processes of time. There is the new love that annihilates the old; the mentor sacrificed for progress; the nest emptied and so much more. There is nothing to be done about the pain. It is inevitable.

So it is that eventually, the blows we've levied as surely as those we have received go beyond mere bruising. They break skin. And if we are lucky to live long enough, crack us open.

A tender green shoot rooted deep in our hearts is watered by our pity—for self and for others. Despite the harsh conditions, it grows. This is mercy.

DISASSEMBLING

We tend to think of solitude as refuge—the place to go in order to feel peaceful. When I was younger, I needed just such a place to recharge my batteries because, carrying as many responsibilities as I did, I had to do whatever it took to hold it together. Now that I have been relieved of my obligations—some by choice, some by force—I am free, at last, to disassemble.

This is a noble struggle but a dreadful one, the worn pieces of me scattering about where they are left to lie. On those days I have courage enough to let it be, the tears come. The same tears I once believed held the potential to drown me, now flow freely as a balm, mending rifts that not only go back to the pain that began with my birth, but for the generations that came before and that will come after. I did not know it to be possible to be broken to pieces, and yet get up, get dressed and take a walk, sip a cup of tea. In pieces, there is no plan, no goal. When did I grow brave enough to let myself just fall apart? In this portable solitude, there is no performing, no judgment, no act, manipulation, or tricks. There is no glue.

I struggle, yes. But this struggle transpires on hallowed ground. I meander through inner and outer landscapes, grieving the past. Now that I'm finally beyond holding on, I am faced with the pressing questions age issues to us. "Can I accept even this?" "Can I love myself no matter what?"

THE SOURCE

Now that the external demands on me have receded and my inner universe has become my life work, I am plummeting through layers of protection, like it or not. Some days, I do not feel this as progress, although surely it is, but as falling apart.

Fatigue can be close to the surface on these days, looking a lot like boredom: a lack of will, purpose, and drive. Lethargy breaks out in beads of meaninglessness, a chilled fever bringing my temperature dangerously low. It's a warning sign to pick oneself up and throw one's self back into the heat of life. But it takes even greater courage to instead refrain from whipping one's self into action, forcing vitality, to instead allow oneself to disassemble.

One senses sadness and its close cousin anger struggling to crack through, and one worries about falling into the void. But these are not just the wounds of the child who has never fully healed from parents who disappointed, bullies who transgressed, events that stung, and narratives that burned. This is also the general but no less acute sorrow that the world as a whole has to be quite so out of control. And so, at long last, the void it is.

This is a hard-won benefit of age: the freedom to face the many ways in which one has been wronged—to shout to God that one has always and continues to deserve better. One deserves to live in a better, kinder world, to be loved unconditionally. One deserves to be respected.

No need to act on this anger, to defuse, resolve, or quell it, either. Rather, one can shiver oneself fully alive with the sheer passion of it—authentic emotions that simultaneously burn and heal, fueled by as much truth as one can stand.

PROTEST

I do not have nor need many friends, but the ones I have are precious to me. So when one asks me to lunch to tell me she is moving to Paris to live near her daughter, of course I am happy for her. But my heart protests.

Even now, I can feel her excitement mount as she prepares her home for the move—the living room in which we once talked endlessly about favorite books over tea. There are boxes everywhere. She has already gifted me with several Mertons and Nouwens. I've placed them on my desk, although the very sight of them breaks my heart.

I have shared some of my regret, of course, but am still trying my best to call upon my highest, most generous self, to hold to platitudes with not even a hint of the tragedy that is the truth of it for me. She is all excitement, rightfully so, as she pictures herself at a sidewalk café with her daughter, sipping cappuccinos.

I understand the reasonableness of her going as well as the place her leaving takes in the parade of losses that accompany aging. I would prefer to throw myself at her weeping with abandonment, begging her to stay: a raging storm of protest.

But I don't.

FOR ST. JOSEPH

Perhaps because my dear friend is leaving to live near her daughter in Paris, all of my senses are honed to a point of pain. I spot one of her favorite umbrellas poking out of a box waiting to be taped shut. I will never see it again.

The life in me rises up in protest, grasping at every detail as if an act of will could freeze this—in fact, every precious moment—in time. I don't like feeling pain, but there is something exquisite about this heightened degree of passion, too.

My youngest grandson, earlier today, tossed a book into my lap and demanded that he be read to. I am too slow for him, sticky fingers competing with mine to turn the page. My older grandson, earphones blocking out the chatter, listening to a book on his phone. I have to tap him on the arm, first lightly, then firmly, to capture his attention long enough to say goodbye for the day. When I do, he surprises me, throwing his arms around me. But of course, even this is transitory.

I leave their home as I left my friend's apartment, followed by wandering through the grocery store then around the block with three shuffling dogs. I am a hungry ghost, already feeling the hopelessness of holding onto what is already the past, all the while cherishing the poignant passion of the present moment: the twin souls of love and pain.

I feel it in every perfectly ripe heirloom tomato, in the furry black ears on Molly scanning like antennas, and our oldest dog Sammy's impossibly crooked tail. It's even in the bottle of St. Joseph's Children's Aspirin I picked up at the pharmacy, a remedy I recall fondly from my childhood—recently prescribed to protect my heart. But life, today, offers no protection.

GREAT ADVENTURE

I am many things today that I wasn't even a couple of months, let alone years ago. I am wiser, more self-nurturing. I understand more about what it means to love and be loved, and how to tender compassion without strings attached. And yet, on any given day, I may also be devastated at some point, ecstatic at another; and the rest, I am often just doing, well, whatever.

At my best, I suppose I am in that state for which I have so mightily striven over the years: Simply living in the present moment. But since the whole point of "being here now" is devoid of commentary or concern, there is quite simply no witness to render judgment—happy or sad. Meaningful or not. And all of this came about not because I ascended into the light, but rather I was finally willing to dive into the shadows to take an honest inventory of myself and the nature of life.

When we finally surrender to age as a time of descent rather than of shoring up, our first thought is that there will now be no end to the darkness. What courage it takes to jump off the edge of who we once thought we were and plunge headfirst into the shadows. We brace ourselves for encounters with old wounds, aspects of ourselves and others we judge to be incorrigible. We expect our broken hearts, so poorly patched, to burst open again and we shudder at the thought of what awaits.

But at last there comes an end to it. And what a surprise when at the very bottom we are met not with a crash, but silence. There is no horizon large enough to contain the enormity of it. And from the infinite depths, a wee voice, whispers: "But ah, what a great adventure this life we're having!"

When we finally surrender to age as a time of descent rather than of shoring up, our first thought is that there will now be no end to the darkness.

But at last there comes an end to it. And what a surprise when at the very bottom we are met not with a crash, but silence. And from the silence, a wee voice, whispers:

"But ah, what a great adventure this life we're having!"

VI
FIERCE WITH AGE
Growing not only old but whole

GRAND GESTURE

As we become older, wiser, and fiercer, we learn to accept that even in our awakened state, we are still not calling the shots. This turns out to be a good thing. Only by admitting to the crumbling of the illusion of our mastery and taking into account what we now know to be the truth about our own and human nature can we begin the critical work of providing a stronger basis upon which a more authentic relationship to life can be built.

When we give up trying to control our outcomes, here's where the real work of conscious aging begins. First, we renounce our thoughts, our patterns, our addictions. These may not be so easily dismissed, but they can with practice increasingly come to be witnessed rather than engaged. Seeing the stories that once conscribed our lives for what they are, we admit to the whole truth. We are far more capable, loveable, and knowledgeable than we gave ourselves credit for. We are—each and every one of us—mad, glorious, passionately alive spirits who are called to celebrate that we have what it takes to have come this far. Regardless of our circumstances, we can tender compassion to ourselves—our loveable essence. Then what? You trust yourself, trust God, to do what comes spontaneously. Maybe just pause—that's a choice, too. Allowing presence to hold and heal you for as long as it takes.

We are always free to make a better choice. But ultimately, one finds that the choice is not happiness versus unhappiness, but rather choosing to live in as meaningful a way as possible, come what may.

BEYOND RESIGNATION

For nearly the entire decade of midlife, we are unsure how much time and energy to invest in keeping our looks youthful, our bodies supple, our world expanding. And when it is early enough to believe we still have even the slightest chance of succeeding at it, we try, then over time, try harder yet to offset what, if left to nature's devices, would be the organic process of growing old.

For those of us brave enough to walk through the gate to old age with eyes wide open, eventually we get to see not only the wrinkles and unsteady gait—we can gain second sight.

Call it character—that mix of acceptance, courage, and perseverance that for many of us grows in tandem with the losses. However you name it, there can come a day when we recognize we're changed, but feel only the sense of relief that, beyond resignation, one can take comfort in who we have become. We come to take private delight in ourselves just as one comes to prefer a handmade vase of flowers from one's own garden over the designer bouquet meant for show. That is how, in the end, one comes to appreciate greatness and beauty in the old and infirm without recoil or dismissal, having been reduced by a long life to one's better self.

BECOMING YOURSELF

How sobering, that moment when we come to realize that we are capable of a peculiar greatness. As we grow over time into our unique, authentic self, what others think of us becomes less and less of a concern. We lose our filters and find words issuing forth that may not be judicious, but are certainly honest.

Others may one day stumble across us as if we were benevolent orbs, shedding light like the spring sun. But on other days, they will find us raging like a winter storm, unleashed and unrepentant. Whatever they may encounter, we will be neither rewarding nor punishing, teaching nor modeling. It is as though we will have become forces of nature, something with which others must deal. At our age, this very triumph of the spirit is what can be dismissed as "eccentric" or "cranky." But this marginalization is the very means by which we evolve into the highest form of our unique variation of being.

What it actually takes to live authentically comes as a revelation, given that the knife that cuts us off so painfully is the very knife that rids us of that which we no longer want or need in our lives. What remains is formidable! But still, we must remind ourselves, when we succeed at this, we are not being difficult. We are simply being ourselves.

FLOODED

The best part of writing is the moment just before I pick up my pen. In the silence of sweet anticipation, there is the only perfection I know: believing that whatever it is I'm experiencing amounts to something. Perhaps not to be shared, but that can make it even sweeter.

I am a writer, embraced by prayer. Even before there are words for it, I trust enough in myself, in life, to believe I can make sense of the stories in my brain, the drumbeat of feelings in my heart, the spontaneous acts of kindness and emotional hurricanes. There's the gentle breeze of grieving completed and the lapping waves of sadnesses that will never end. And, too, the simultaneous effort to capture the unearned ecstasy of freedom and joy. In other words: creation, art, love.

Before my pen ever touches the paper, I can feel the tears behind my eyes. But are these tears of joy? Or sorrow? Both? Neither? By the time I'm through I'll have words for it, but they will always fall short. For it is in the intimate silence where hope is gestated and prayer is born that I truly get it right.

SACRED IDENTITY

Is this too good to be true? To sit by the river with my journal in hand, feeling so deeply connected. It is like a wisp, faint, but strong: a spider's web that looks like smoke but could lift a mountain. I sense the filaments entwining my heart and I begin to weep. I am rising to the occasion that growing older, wiser, fiercer has called forth from me. Not only the challenges of age, but life, itself.

Just as Kabbalists are amongst those who cannot speak aloud the name of God, this sense of connection to something greater than oneself is always to be found on the very next page—holding the promise of a transcendent merger that defies anything as small as a name.

It is in this spirit that I speak well—even fondly— of the remnants of my persisting discontent as an awareness of the distance between points: the tacit acknowledgement that, in fact, both the realized and the possible actually do exist.

Tears flow freely, as if a huge burden has been lifted—perhaps by the filaments of simplicity I'd sensed in this moment of river, web, and sunlight: a wholeness not dependent on making things happen or anything even remotely related to ambition.

My journal demands nothing of me. It receives just what I am willing to give, and rewards me with insights about myself and the world I inhabit. I am content, feeling the warmth on the page and the ink flow from the pen, but then an unexpected breeze turns the page flying and a new moment arrives.

THIS PATCH

One of the greatest gifts of later life is that we can grow to become not nearly as fascinated with our original wounds as we used to be. It's not that we don't sometimes feel we weren't loved the way we deserved. But, by now, we've run this storyline so many times, it's become boring—even to ourselves.

Of course, confronting our shadows is still one giant step up from denial. But somewhere along the line—if we are lucky—we realize that while the process of spiritual growth does indeed necessitate opening to old wounds, that's just step one. After we have sucked the juice out of them. we are meant to get on with it.

Growing up spiritually doesn't mean you don't ever again experience old, familiar places of sadness, anger, jealousy, fear, and despair. But when you do, you know yourself well enough to trust that you do not need to take up permanent residency. Here, in our new life stage, we at last get to experience the freedom beyond our childhood traumas and discover what it means to make fresh, life-affirming choices for ourselves.

I can assure you, this letting go of the engagement with your original wounds feels counterintuitive at first. But there comes a time when the sheer magnitude of who you really are and what you have made of your life can no longer be circumscribed by the size of your story. You arrive at last into the realm of the awakened elder for whom over lunch, on the phone, on long walks, the conversation has changed—dramatically.

Yes, the hits keep coming, but no longer does every transgression need be assigned a villain; nor does every disappointment trigger the need to reassert control. In fact, the things we encounter while we're living our lives no longer inspire accusations and victimhood, nor self-mortification. And that's when things get really interesting!

Then what? What do we have to talk about with one another? How about just holding hands as we walk this next patch of life together as a prayer: cry when we must, laugh too, and if we have to say anything at all, let it be *Amen.*

CLAIMING JOY

Who amongst us does not know more now than we did ten, thirty, or fifty years ago . . . not just about what is right and what is wrong, but who we are and the nature of the choices that are ours to make?

We have been informed by dreams and nightmares as well as by unearned grace. There has been inspiration in the words of others who came before lighting the path to inner wisdom. Too, there are elders who are still with us, walking just a step ahead with dignity and grace, even if on shuffling feet.

Somehow, we established our own pace, all

judgments about having skipped ahead or fallen behind, proving to be temporary. Crisis by crisis, we replaced false and untrue bits of ourselves with that for which we always sought: not the simple joy to which the child thought she was entitled, but joy, nevertheless.

Do I dare call this embrace of my own complexity "joy"? Yes, this is joy—joy born of surrender and acceptance, paradoxically co-existing in one heart with hope, aspiration and pain. This paradox defies the rational and forces me open-eyed into faith. At once awe-full and awe-some, even the finding, losing, and recovery of faith is part and parcel to the joy I can now claim as my own.

SILENCE

The recognition that I prefer to live in my small self came late in life and I would not now trade it for anything. Growing old helps slow me down, limits options, provides cover for the tenderest parts of myself. Small is where I am grounded, nourished, whole. Digging deep into these new-found sensitivities, I find myself capable of stopping mid-sentence, taking refuge in silence. In this state, alone even when others are present, I can be perfectly fine.

If I encounter someone while I am in this state, I may share a smile, but I no longer feel the need to perform, justify or explain my existence. I listen, I appreciate. I muse. I would have once judged one such as this as dull. But in this place, where being complete is purpose enough, I can look admiringly at the life teeming about me grounded, enduring: the immutable rock in the river and no longer the driven salmon.

This is not a ploy, an enhanced attempt at eliciting care or attention. The truth is, what I have discovered is that no one minds or even notices, and I am now more often than not delighted to be getting away with it.

HOUSEBOAT

Dan and I shared in the decision to buy our little houseboat, but we view our boat differently. Dan sees it as a vehicle for adventure, captain of the high seas, although with an old engine that burns hot, we don't go far from shore. Because of the boat, we have transformed Nashville's summers from something to dread into a thing of wonder: water-cooled breezes, outrunning mosquitoes, and soaring beneath lyrically-winged blue herons.

But in the winter, the boat is all mine. I do not need to turn on the engine or even untether the lines to be transported into a simpler time and place. I have a little heater and a steamer to make hot tea. With sky over the bow and a roof over the cabin, I am free either to feel the cleansing winter mist on my face, or to snuggle safe and dry beneath as many blankets as I'd wish. When the rain comes, it bounces noisily off the roof and rolls down the windows, lightning and thunder putting on quite the show.

Bundling up on the stern, close to the water line, I see a fish leaping skyward through half-closed eyes. The slice of silver propels itself high into the air, then I hear her splash against the surface with a round burst of spray that rings in my delighted ears.

ECLIPSE

On the day of the total solar eclipse, we set out for our little houseboat with friends and dogs, imagining ourselves toasting totality in the middle of the lake.

Then the boat wouldn't start. While Dan turned the key and the engine pinged metallically, my spirit left my body to plunge deep into fifty years of disappointments, frustrations, and shortcomings taken personally, unfairly or not.

Meanwhile, Dan was patiently, diligently, methodically turning the key, as again and again, he summoned forth nary more than a pathetic click, click, click. But what was this? Laughing? The six of them were fine. "No worries," our guests reassured us. "The eclipse will be everywhere—at sea, on shore, in the slip. All we need to do is look up."

Just then, the engine kicked in: full throated, powerful, life-giving. We cheered, we hugged, we sped to the middle of the lake and into the joyously darkening sky.

WONDERFULLY MADE

What does one make of hope when we see how many attempts we've made to improve ourselves, only to remain essentially the same? The same tendencies, traits, and habits we'd thought we'd beaten into submission re-emerge again, sometimes subtler, but essentially unchanged.

It is not that our lives don't improve. Eventually, one learns not to give voice to every impulse—how to avoid situations that trigger our worst and to instead seek out people and circumstances that allow us to shine. But we cannot avoid the truth that the unique combination of qualities and characteristics—that essential essence that makes one a "me"—is so often merely being managed and corralled. It is either foolishness or heroism to believe that one's personality can be changed.

And yet, I believe. Not that I will ever be able to significantly separate from the "me" that persists through time and space. But that I can get better at telling the truth about who I am—comprised as I am of both the shadow and light; that I can lovingly witness the interplay between impulse and control; and that I can come to trust God that while I may never be perfect, I was wonderfully made.

It takes courage to dive deeply into the barriers and complexities of what it takes to become one's authentic self.

We must look to our shadow, reclaiming much of what we'd denied about ourselves and our lives and jettisoning previously useful aspects that we've outgrown.

But at last, there comes an end to it And we realize that in becoming more fully ourselves, we were not just being difficult. We were becoming whole.

VII
THAT I MAY SMILE AGAIN
When Life Matters Most

DOGGY STEPS

Our two oldest dogs, little Sammy and Lucky, can—on a good day—pick their way up the doggie steps to the sofa. Reaching their favorite spots, they curl up exhausted after prevailing upon their hind legs to finally obey and the whole dog gratefully makes it over the edge onto the cushion. When they get there at last, they rest content. At that exact moment, Molly, our youngest dog at a relatively spry 9, bounds up right past them with such velocity and strength, all of them—including Molly—seem a bit startled to see that she has missed the steps entirely, having arrived at her destination in one grand leap.

On any given day, I'm not entirely sure which dog I'm going to be: old dog or spry dog. In most regards, however, this is less worrisome than it once was as I've become adjusted to taking my energy as it comes, day by day. Then I joined an aerobics dance class nearby, only to discover that I had inadvertently become part of a chorus line, sandwiched between high-kickers. It was only when my eyes were closed that I thought I was keeping up. The deafening drumbeat and relentless mirror could be fierce taskmasters, indeed, as it was my ego—not my ability—that forced me to hold it together. At the end of class, light-headed and relieved that no one had gone flying on account of me, I dragged myself home, willing my legs to take that last step to sofa's edge.

Now, instead, I walk. Taking pride in having made such a good decision, I set my own pace, for as long as I feel invigorated rather than drained. This varies from day to day, so requires equal amounts of consciousness and truth-telling. In inclement weather, I walk the treadmill at the gym. But the dogs and I live for those blessed days when we can leash ourselves up and take a walk around the neighborhood. Cloudy and crisp; sun-warmed and toasty, refreshing drizzle: our spirits revive and we come home just tired enough.

Some days, one or another of the dogs simply cannot make it onto the sofa without help. If Dan or I fail to notice, he or she may be found, who knows how many minutes later, standing patiently if dumbfounded, front paws on the top step, back paws frozen a step behind. This is what worries me about my own aging. When despite the strength of my will, the things I want cannot flex to my shifting needs, but require some minimal level of physical competence that is eluding me. I worry about the future, anticipating the day that someone finds me patient but dumb-founded, standing stock still at the bottom of the stairs.

THE FRIENDLY MIRROR

I woke up this morning and there was an old woman staring back at me. So I pulled out every jar, stick, and tube and then there she was: an old woman wearing make-up. I rummaged through the closet and found an old favorite hat to put on. Ah ha! I said when I had positioned it at a jaunty angle. And now there was an old woman wearing a great hat.

Over the next few minutes, there was much rummaging and adjusting and soon there was an old woman wearing sunglasses and a signature scarf. But with all the layers and manipulations, nothing had altered the truth of the matter. I am a woman. I am old. And I am out of tricks.

But I am not out of choices. I could choose to continue to fret, regretting the loss of my youthful looks. Or I could choose to think of myself as beautiful for my age. Or—and this one was new—I could take it all in, have a good laugh, then get on with it.

The minute this third option crossed my mind, my face changed completely. I no longer searched for a particular blush of beauty in the reflection, but rather, I saw everything I had ever been, could, or will be: the good, the bad, the beautiful, the ugly, everything in between, and something beyond it all and, breathing in every single bit of it, I was taken aback. This face was not only hard-worn but hard-won, so in less time than it had taken to put it all on, most of it came right off and the bit that remained was just right.

I turned away from the suddenly friendly mirror, no longer fighting growing old—nor accepting it. I was just me again. And isn't that what I'd been searching for all along?

FALLIBLE

I am finally coming to terms with the fallibility of the human condition. Beneath the superficial differences that individuate us—as multifarious as these may be—there is a template to the trajectory of our lives that transcends centuries, geographies, and religious differences. In fact, I am coming to believe that all of art, literature, creativity, commerce, politics— maybe everything—are the manifestations of people struggling each in his or her own way to break through to making sense of things.

And what is this truth we all share, the enigma that breaks the universal code? We're mortal. So simple. So self-evident. But this is not what I'd expected to hear when I prayed so long and diligently for deliverance.

Behind this final mask is the heart of the thing that has now stuck with me: surrender to my own fallibility. And it is only by God's grace that, at least today, I do not feel only shame at the hubris of my failed attempts at immortality, but relief. I can at last pack up the self-defense circus and just take my spot in the lineup alongside all the other clowns, fools, and reprobates that make up the human race.

Nothing of this means I can't still experience joy or do good although I now know there are no guarantees. I feel unremarkably ordinary and, for the moment, it is somehow okay.

FIELD OF LOVE

Another of the great gifts of age is that perceptions—
even cherished ones—can seemingly change in a
flash. All the life experience, all the trial and error, all
the observation and contemplation finally amounts
to something. It is as if each of us has a spiritual
Rosetta Stone: a touch-point that unlocks the key to
freedom. For some, it's acceptance. For others, it's
fulfillment. For me—for many of us—it's love.
Although one can certainly touch the state I'm
getting at through loving relationship, I'm thinking
more of existential love: an ultimate destination from
whence we come and to which we will return. I

picture this as a vast field of love, both personal and transcendent: a place of unity with the universe where your individual story recedes, and your heart breaks open with clarity and compassion for, well, everything.

I know that many of us have glimpses of the field of love, but most consider these transcendent moments to be treasured exceptions rather than the rule, as if the love and beauty of life is something scarce that comes and goes, and is, at best, a sneak preview of coming attractions. But what if the truth is that we never left the field of love that we envision as both preceding and awaiting us? What if it just feels like we pass the bulk of our days on less luminous terrain because for a number of logical, inevitable reasons, we're blocked? Like standing in a field in the bright noon sun but with eclipse glasses on.

So what if the field of love is not something you left behind or are going toward? What if it's not an exception but everywhere? All the time. Right here. If you were to take off your glasses, right now, you know what you'd see? All those folks who you wished wouldn't have to be quite so bad are just a bunch of people standing around in the field with you, with their shades on. You will only know your own glasses are off when you can look at the dysfunction all around you and simultaneously experience grief and compassion. And what's this? You will recognize others scattered about whose glasses have already been tossed off, who have been waiting patiently for you.

The external world may not ever change its storyline, but you are now free to cease preoccupying yourself with all the apparently unloving stuff that's happened to you and to others, and see beyond your own compelling but tertiary story as well. The mystics put it like this. Consider the possibility that spirituality is not just a way to alleviate the problem of being human with sporadic moments of transcendence. Rather, you are made of the very same stuff as the field of love itself.

So that's everything. The story of our lives and the truth of things. Not a matter to be defended, compared, or exalted. Not just a place we've come from and are heading toward. Rather, we are here. We are now. And whether your glasses are on or off, distorted, thick, or too dark to see through presently, love is standing by.

STRAY

Today, all is simple and clear—as if there were never any confusion no complexity regarding God, meaning, or the nature of life. Of course, it's easier to feel close to God on days like today, warmed to perfection by a light spring breeze, nothing particularly wrong or unpleasant. The dogs are draped on chaise lounges, deck chairs, and one dog—Lucky—is once again sitting in stiff attention at the base of a tree: squirrel watch.

Sammy's head is resting on my lap. Sammy, our sweet Maltese whose owner passed on and the children wouldn't keep him. He was found by a local dog sanctuary wandering on a highway and, by God's grace, found his way to our home. At 13, Sammy is missing teeth, so he nuzzles morsels from our hands. When we first saw him, he was scruffy, with bare patches and a crooked tail. He's looking better now that he's benefited from good nutrition, professional grooming, and a lot of petting. Through everything he's endured, he has not forgotten love or gratitude. After a first night shaking in our laps he now runs outdoors with the other dogs, lines up for treats, and wags his crooked tail when we re-enter a room.

He came to us with no more history than I've described, but we are learning gradually that not only is he a loving dog, but somewhere along the line, he must also have been well-loved. When he wants something, he knows that his vocal demand is likely to be heeded, but to stifle his bark so as to not unduly disturb. The sound emits like a huff— firm but respectful. By means of huffing, he commandeered a place on our bed with the others so that I now sleep with right leg crooked around Molly, Lucky is between Dan and I at one of my ears, and Sammy is at the other. All night long I feel him whispering his secrets to me. One can hardly imagine—does not want to—the terror of being cast out, an 8-pound lap dog left to fight for his life in a world that can be as cruel and unfair as it can be gracious and loving.

Sammy's whispers are still with me—I have brought them to this blessed day, in which uniting with God seems so simple. This is what I hear. "If God is one, then God is in everything, everywhere. God must be as much in the things that sadden, anger and disappoint us as God is in the good. But what kind of God is this who is present in both shadow and light?"

Today, the answer is simple and clear. For where are faith, mercy, and forgiveness found but in the shadows? God is not the source of evil, but surely, God is with us in our responses to those things that cause us pain, anger and sorrow. Even after all these years seeking God, it has barely been enough time to process a God this great, who overlooks nothing, offering grace to all. But small is the exact place to which I have been called, myself but a stray who has exhausted every other possible option, only to find herself whispering in God's ear "How great the mystery. How great the love."

NEXT BREATH

Live long and well enough, then someday—
seemingly out of nowhere, rising like a phoenix from
the ashes—you will be swept with unexpected
tenderness for yourself and for others: the whole
human drama in which you have given life more than
you knew you had in you, but it was still not enough.
Only then, when your ego has been shattered and
who you once thought you were has turned to dust,
can you finally see and accept the love—flawed as it
may have been–that had been there all along. We
recognize the embers of goodness and meaning that
have persisted despite everything, glowing through

the ashes of our failed expectations. We recall all of it, leave nothing out, and at the very moment we embrace the imperfection of it all, we are redeemed.

Of course, as the narratives about life and death tend to go, it would be most elegant if all this happened to coincide with our last breath. Isn't this the ultimate culmination—the simultaneous confession and deliverance? It's easier that way, dissolving into joy and the redemption of meaning along with your final exhale without having to give yourself time and opportunity to screw up again. But why work so hard for psycho-spiritual liberation well before one's last breath if there were no hope of awakening from illusion earlier over the course of our lives, with time to spare?

It's not easy. It's not elegant. But it is possible. Moment by moment: you have over- or underestimated your strength; you over- or underestimated your bad habits; there's something else to try; there is no cure. The imperfections still sting; the lack of control still vexes; the successes still inflate; the guilt and grief remain potent. Even so, you can wake up—long before your last breath. But to stay awake, you would have to forgive yourself, forgive it all, accept it all, love it all over and over again in real time.

I have been graced with a great gift, having stumbled across the awakened hearts of others, crying out in pain and joy; and I am simultaneously breaking open and healing my own heart along the way. I write this, as vulnerable, grateful, and fresh as I have ever been, inhabiting my life and my world awake just enough to know that something is over for me that I will miss terribly but do not want back.

ARRIVAL

It just happened again. I woke up feeling every bit my age, careening toward my morning shower—when I was swept with joy because I love my shower curtain. I love my shampoo. I love that I can trust that the spray will come out at the exact warmth and intensity I prefer.

Eight years ago, at the age of 63 when I was fraught with the challenges of growing old in our ageist, dysfunctional society, I vowed to transform myself from victim to explorer. I viewed the far side of midlife as wild territory, full of dangerous unknowns, and saw that my mission as a participant/observer would be to report back my discoveries. Happy to say, I believe that I'm making headway, even if some of what I've encountered has required a greater degree of hacking away through thorny brush with a duller machete than I would have hoped.

I have to admit that fraught is not an accidental choice of words but the most accurate way to describe my mood for much of this journey. The early stretch was the most difficult, where you still believe that if you just try hard enough, you can stop the more serious effects of aging from happening to you. But only when the irreversible losses begin setting in and it is clear there's no turning back do you become a candidate for serious transformation.

One can learn to reap the benefits of aging, but there is an investment to be made, and it is rarely pain free. One must also do the challenging philosophical, religious, and spiritual work of coming to terms with the world, questions of ultimate concern, and the human condition as well as the difficult therapeutic work of making peace with one's past. There are issues of legacy to be attended to, disillusionments to be faced, amends to be made, and self-love to be administered. Much of this journey into the unknown is harrowing, some of it transcendent and most of it unexpected.

But there comes a time when the fraught nature of the work is done, even while growth continues apace. For those who live long enough to transit beyond transition to transformation, eventually—mercifully—spiritual growth no longer centers on the metaphor of a heart broken open, but rather, on a heart grown whole. There is, at last, not only the fraught journey through older age—but an arrival.

HEAD-FIRST

I used to think the best one could hope for from dying was a gentle fading away. I believed this to be true in my late forties, when I was diagnosed with breast cancer, placed myself in God's tender care, and survived. Somehow, I managed to get past making deals and beyond offering up sacrifices and when healing came about, I did not take credit.

But now, more than twenty years later, with death no longer untimely but inevitable, I find myself face to face with yet another paradox of age. While I am even more at peace with my mortality, I heartily reject the notion of a slow fade. There is little about me in how I live my life that is about fading away into anything and I now hope to be fully, fiercely me to the very end. If you are poking at me and it makes me mad, I hope to not be forcing myself to tell jokes. If making demands and resisting arbitrary orders makes me difficult, so be it. I plan, too, to save some of my choicest words for God. But in all honesty, if at the moment of my passing I am feeling blessedly serene, that would have to be alright, too.

Whatever it is I am to have become at the very end, I hope to be feeling as honest, curious, adventurous, and passionate about life through my last exhale as I do today. Being fully alive means being open to surprises—and when it comes right down to it, what choice do we really have? And so it is I hope that at the end, I am reluctant to let go, having learned at long last to love every bit of this whole crazy, challenging, wonderful, fierce experience that has comprised my unique and particular life. But then, when it is absolutely clear there's to be no turning back, that for which I hope most fiercely is not a slipping away but rather a spectacular dive head first at the last possible second, eyes and heart wide open.

ONE WHITE CRANE

We who are old did not ask to be tested by time, to learn through our suffering or to become heroes. We would rather life had not asked quite so much of us—presented even a few less occasions to which we had to rise.

Yet but one white crane dipping and soaring above the river can do much to alleviate the weight of sacrifices made along the way. Some losses were offered up. Others were suffered. At 71, I have finally let go, but I am not empty. Rather, I am overflowing with more emotions than I know what to do with.

At once grieving and celebrating—age-appropriate and well-earned. Is this the final gate though which we must pass to find wisdom? And what is this we find at the end of our journey? *How magnificent this life we're living, if only we let it be.*

AFTERWORD
WORK OF ART
Robert L. Weber, Ph.D.

Life is full of paradox. Four years ago, Carol Orsborn and I launched the book we co-authored, *The Spirituality of Age: A Seeker's Guide to Growing Older,* at The Harvard Bookstore. Our book confronts the shadow side of aging, finding spiritual opportunity in the challenges—including physical losses—associated with growing older. After working together for nearly 4 years, it was a night to celebrate the hard, long-distance collaboration that birthed our book. But as Carol Orsborn, in this insightful new selection of her essays, *Older, Wiser, Fiercer: The Wisdom Collection*, will be quick to remind you, even under the best of circumstances, growing older represents a disruption of how things used to be. "Any day can bring with it the realization that we do not have the power either to make things turn out how we'd expected, nor go back the way they were," writes Carol.

And so it was that by the time our book tour took us to Nashville, I could barely stand for the presentation. Two weeks earlier, I'd injured myself during a Pilates exercise. Strain and pain took possession of my left hip and the symptoms continued with little relief. Subsequently, my condition was diagnosed as degenerative arthritis and osteoarthritis requiring hip replacement surgery. But that would have to wait, for, by tour's end, just one month later, I was diagnosed with prostate cancer that also required surgery. This was a challenging time, to say the least, one in which I was hastened by circumstances to not only write about the paradox of aging, but to find myself doing first-hand, deeper research about the spiritual opportunities that occur not in spite of, but because of aging. In her work of timeless wisdom, *The Measure of Our Days,* Florida Scott-Maxwell refers to this stance as becoming *fierce with reality.* But as it turns out, despite the gifts aging brings to us, the shadow side informs us that there can also be such a thing as *too much reality.*

Carol's ongoing journey led to her literary connection and dialogue with the work of wise elders from across a broad spectrum of eras and disciplines, writers like Scott-Maxwell, May Sarton, and Joan Chittister, even as my own journey has taken me deeper into the work of others that Carol appreciates as well, especially the teachings of Richard Rohr and Ignatius of Loyola. Through our reading and ongoing conversations, Carol and I have continued both our individual and mutually supportive quests for answers, trying to make sense of our aging and the meaning and opportunities that are part of this universally inevitable process.

I am proud to call Carol Orsborn not only my coauthor, but my friend. I have long admired both her passion for living: the ability to lay bare the truth of mortality while determined to live life to the full. Writes Carol: "I hope to feel as honest, raw, passionate about life through my last exhale as I do today. No slow fade, but rather, when it is absolutely clear there's no turning back, a spectacular dive head first at the last possible second, eyes and heart wide open."

In his Introduction to Carol's latest work, our friend Rick Moody refers to the notion of "spaete Werke", recognizing that what the elder artists disclosed through paint, writers like Carol Orsborn disclose to us through words. I couldn't agree more. Like docents who open our eyes to the beauty of art, she opens our eyes to the beauty of artful aging. Reading Carol's newest collection will inspire you to grow into your authentic self. I can think of no more apt way to mark the installation of *Older, Wiser, Fiercer* than with this quote by Eleanor Roosevelt: "Beautiful young people are accidents of nature, but beautiful old people are works of art."

ACKNOWLEDGMENTS

To my children and grandchildren and our extended and growing family, for sharing life and love with me and providing endless entertainment.

To my soul circle of friends, theologians, and guides, including Bob Weber, Rick Moody, Leanne Flask, Emily Askew, Jill Speering, Pat Halper, Judith Wolf-Mandell, Shana Mackler, Lj Ratliff, Susan Underwood, Brent Green, John C. Robinson, and Connie Goldman, for gifting me with the understanding that we can not only grow old, but whole.

To all those of us who are growing older, wiser, and fiercer together including the *Fierce with Age* and *Conscious Aging Book Club* communities as well as my dream group and tai chi, chi gong, and yoga buddies at Fifty Forward, Madison Station, Tennessee.

Most of all, to my husband Dan, my Beshert.
You have my deepest appreciation and respect.

APPENDICES

BIOGRAPHIES

Carol Orsborn, Ph.D.

Dr. Carol Orsborn is the best-selling author of over 30 books including 2015 Gold Nautilus Book Award winner in the category of Consciously Aging: *The Spirituality of Age: A Seeker's Guide to Growing Older* (with Robert L. Weber, Ph.D.)

She received her Doctorate in History and Critical Theory of Religion from Vanderbilt University, specializing in adult development and ritual studies, including intergenerational values formation and transmission. She has served on the adjunct faculties of Pepperdine, Loyola Marymount, and Georgetown Universities. She is currently curator of *Fierce with Age: The Archives of Boomer Wisdom, Inspiration, and Spirituality* .

For the past forty years, Dr. Orsborn has been a leading voice of her generation, appearing on *Oprah*, *NBC Nightly News*, and on *The Today Show* among many others. Her blogs have appeared regularly in *Huffington Post*, *Beliefnet*, and NPR's *Next Avenue*, among others. She has been a frequent speaker at conferences and events such as the American Society of Aging, Sage-ing International Conference, Boomerstock, the Positive Aging Conference, Omega Institute, and the American Academy of Religion, and has been a featured presenter multiple times with the Shift Network.

Dr. Orsborn established her reputation as a generational expert as co-founder of Fleishman-Hillard's FM Boom, the first global initiative by a top ten PR company dedicated to helping brands such as Ford, AARP, Prudential, and Humana communicate with Boomers.

Dr. Orsborn lives in Nashville, Tennessee as part of an extended grand-family including three beloved dogs.

Harry R. Moody, Ph.D.

Dr. Moody is Distinguished Visiting Professor, Creative Longevity, and Wisdom Program, Fielding Graduate University, as well as emeritus director of

Academic Affairs and Vice President for AARP. He is the author of numerous books and articles including the classic *The Five Stages of the Soul.*

His other titles include: *Abundance of Life: Human Development Policies for an Aging Society, Ethics in an Aging Society,* and *Aging: Concepts and Controversies,* a gerontology textbook now in its eighth edition.

A graduate of Yale and holder of a Ph.D. in philosophy from Columbia University, Dr. Moody taught philosophy at Columbia, Hunter College, New York University, and the University of California at Santa Cruz.

From 1999 to 2001 he served as National Program Director of the Robert Wood Johnson Foundation's Faith in Action and, from 1992 to 1999, was executive director of the Brookdale Center at Hunter College. Before coming to Hunter, he served as administrator of Continuing Education Programs for the Citicorp Foundation and later as codirector of the National Aging Policy Center of the National Council on Aging in Washington, DC.

Dr. Moody is known nationally for his work in older adult education and served as Chairman of the Board of Elderhostel.

Robert L. Weber, Ph.D.

Dr. Weber (Bob) is a retired Assistant Professor of Psychology (Harvard Medical School, Department of Psychiatry) and a retired Assistant in Psychology (Massachusetts General Hospital, Department of Psychiatry). A former Jesuit, he is coauthor with Carol Orsborn of *The Spirituality of Age: A Seeker's Guide to Growing Older*, which won the 2015 Nautilus Book Award Gold Medal in the category of Aging Consciously. In 2014 he received the American Society on Aging's FORSA Award (Forum on Religion, Spirituality, and Aging) in recognition of his leadership exploring the role of spirituality and religion in the aging services field.

After graduation from Princeton University, he began a Master of Arts in Teaching program at Harvard University. After his first year of study and teaching in the Harvard program, he entered the Jesuit Province in New England. After the two-year Jesuit novitiate, he returned to Harvard, completed his M.A.T. degree, and, then began and completed a three-year Master of Divinity degree with Distinction at the Weston Jesuit School of Theology.

Dr. Weber lived, worked, and trained as a Jesuit for almost ten years. After much prayer and spiritual direction and discernment, he took a leave of absence from the Order and began doctoral study and training in clinical psychology at Temple University in Philadelphia. After ending his LOA and leaving the Jesuit order, he married and moved back to Boston where he completed a predoctoral internship and postdoctoral fellowship at Massachusetts General Hospital-Harvard Medical School. Once he received his Ph.D. in clinical psychology, he launched a private practice and his career as a psychologist which continues in Cambridge, Massachusetts.

When Dr. Weber entered his mid-fifties, he began a personal and professional journey intended to integrate the three major threads of his life:

psychology, spirituality, and aging. Over time he became an active member of the American Society on Aging and served on the Leadership Council for the Forum on Religion, Spirituality, and Aging. He began giving talks and leading workshops on spirituality, aging, and mental health across the country, work he continues to the present.

In the years following his training, he immersed himself in psychoanalytic and psychodynamic theory and practice, while directing the group program at Cambridge Hospital-Harvard Medical School. In addition, he cofounded a group therapy group practice, developed a new training program for the Northeastern Society for Group Psychotherapy (NSGP), and wrote the group training manual for American Group Psychotherapy Association (AGPA) and the National Register of Certified Group Psychotherapists (NRCGP).

Susan Rios

The cover painting, "Bouquet From The Side Garden," is by internationally beloved artist Susan Rios. A professional artist for more than 35 years, Susan's work has attracted the attention of many noted collectors and celebrities who have added her paintings to their private collection such as Jane Seymour, Mr. & Mrs. Bruce Dern, Priscilla Presley, Phyllis George, Ann Gillian, Sandy Duncan, Shelley Fabres, Andre Agassi, Mr. & Mrs. Brian Wilson, and Mr. & Mrs. Walter Matthau.

An active participant in causes that touch her heart, Susan devotedly supports charities and nationwide organizations, including the Los Angeles Children's Hospital, Saddleback Community Outreach (Orange County), Taylor Family Foundation, Make a Wish Foundation and The Ronald McDonald House of Orange County.

Working out of her studio in Glendale, California, Susan Rios' ability to evoke familiar feelings through her paintings is the hallmark of her work. She is known internationally for her palette of soft, warm colors, inviting viewers to step into a world where one tranquil moment can last an eternity. Largely self-taught, Susan's artistic potential was apparent even as a child. Her love of the outdoors inspired her to begin drawing scenes from nature. Today, she continues to find inspiration in the gentle-hearted beauty of everyday life.

The selection of the painting "Bouquet From The Side Garden" was inspired by this quote from "Beyond Resignation" in *Older, Wiser, Fiercer: The Wisdom Collection.*

There can come a day when we recognize we're changed, but feel only the sense of relief that, beyond resignation, one can take comfort in who we have become. We come to take private delight in ourselves just as one comes to prefer a handmade vase of flowers from one's own garden over the designer bouquet meant for show. That is how, in the end, one comes to appreciate greatness and beauty in the old and infirm without recoil or dismissal, having been reduced by a long life to one's better self.

STAY CONNECTED

Join the conversation about Carol Orsborn's *Older, Wiser, Fiercer: The Wisdom Collection* with added bonus features including expanded versions of the Foreword and Afterword online at CarolOrsborn.com.

If you'd like to read and discuss more books about conscious aging, the Conscious Aging Book Club, led by Carol Orsborn, meets monthly at Parnassus Books, Nashville's top independent book store. The hour-long discussions take place at the Green Hills store, meeting the first Thursday of every month at 10:30 a.m.. (No reservation necessary.) Selections include primarily non-fiction works by experts, mystics, psychologists and authors such as Florida Scott-Maxwell, Ram Dass, Joan Chittister, Zalman Schachter-Shalomi, Connie Goldman, James Hollis, and others.

The CarolOrsborn.com archives also feature highlighted Conscious Aging Book Club selections along with Carol's commentary, discussion prompts, and participant's comments. You are invited to read along and post your thoughts. For a list of these books with links, visit the Book Club tab at CarolOrsborn.com.

To be informed of upcoming selections, please ask to be added to the email list by emailing the Conscious Aging Book Club at Carol@fiercewithage.com with the subject "CABC"

In addition, readers can access Carol Orsborn's sister site *Fierce with Age: The Archives of Boomer Wisdom, Inspiration and Spirituality* at *FierceWithAge.com,* featuring nearly 1000 digest entries, summaries, comments, and links to curated content about conscious aging.

Carol Orsborn can be reached at:
Carol@fiercewithage.com.

RELATED BOOKS BY CAROL ORSBORN

Are You Still Listening? Stories and Essays. With Brent Green et al. Denver, 2019. *Winner National Indie Excellence Awards of the category of Social/Political Change.*

Angelica's Last Breath. Nashville: Fierce with Age Press, 2018.

The Spirituality of Age: A Seeker's Guide to Growing Older. Coauthored with Dr. Robert L. Weber. Inner Traditions, 2015. *Winner of a Gold Nautilus Award in the category of Aging Consciously. Spanish edition by Inner Traditions, 2018.*

Fierce with Age: Chasing God and Squirrels in Brooklyn. Nashville: Turner Publishing, 2013.

The Art of Resilience: 100 Paths to Wisdom and Strength in an Uncertain World. New York: Three Rivers Press/Random House, 1997.

Nothing Left Unsaid: Words to Help You and Your Loved Ones through the Hardest Time. Berkeley, California: Conari Press, 2001.

Boom: Marketing to the Ultimate Power Consumer— the Baby Boomer Woman. With Mary Brown. New York: Amacom Publishing, 2006.

The Silver Pearl: Our Generation's Journey to Wisdom with Dr. Jimmy Laura Smull. Chicago: Ampersand, Inc. 2005

Solved by Sunset: The Self-Guided Intuitive Decision-Making Retreat. New York: Harmony/Random House, 1996 and New York: Crown, 1997.

Speak the Language of Healing: Living with Breast Cancer without Going to War. Foreword by Jean Shinoda Bolen, M.D. With Susan Kuner et al. Berkeley, California: Conari Press, 1997.

Made in the USA
Middletown, DE
30 November 2019

79655229R00113